Taylor's
Dictionary
for Gardeners

Taylor's Dictionary for Gardeners

The definitive guide to the language of horticulture

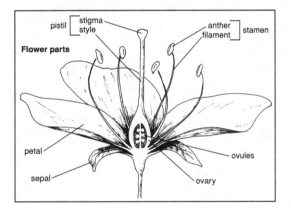

Flower parts

pistil [stigma / style]
anther / filament] stamen
petal
sepal
ovules
ovary

Frances Tenenbaum

HOUGHTON MIFFLIN COMPANY
Boston • New York 1997

Library of Congress Cataloging-in-Publication Data

Tenenbaum, Frances.
    Taylor's dictionary for gardeners / Frances Tenenbaum.
        p.   cm.
    ISBN 0-395-87606-0
    1. Gardening — Dictionaries.   I. Title.
    SB450.95.T45 1997
    635′.03 — dc21   97-23701
                                                      CIP

Printed in the United States of America

QUM 10 9 8 7 6 5 4 3 2 1

Book design by Deborah Fillion
Page layout by Gail Mardfin Starkey

For Alex and Josh

ike every specialized activity or discipline, gardening has a vocabulary of its own. And though gardeners need not be horticulturists, much less botanists, an understanding of the language of gardening is always interesting and often essential. If you don't know what "damping-off" means, the seedlings on your windowsill will likely drop dead. If you can't read a plant label, how will you know whether the nursery's fastigiate pine tree is the right one for your garden?

As gardening gains in popularity and gardeners become more sophisticated, there is a growing trend to dispense with the cute and often misleading names on plant labels and replace them with correct botanical names. This is all to the good, but only if you know what the names mean. And for that, you need to know something about botanical Latin, which is not classical Latin, and which is a lot less intimidating than it sounds. In this dictionary, you'll find the botanical names for most common garden plants, as well as the species names that describe their attributes.

Nor do you have to get far into gardening to be faced with the symbol "pH." Since a simple definition (that pH is a measure of the acidity or alkalinity of soil) is only

marginally helpful, in this dictionary you'll find what the
numbers on the scale mean — that soil with a pH of 5, for
instance, is 10 times more acid than soil with a pH of 6.
You'll also learn the pH range in which plants can be
expected to thrive.

While some of the entries in this dictionary require only a
brief definition (archegonium: the female reproductive organ
of a fern or moss), most contain an explanation that is either
helpful to the practice of gardening or of interest to the
reader. As a gardener, I have known that it is often a good
idea to pinch the growing tip of a newly planted flower to
make it branch out. In researching this dictionary, I learned
about apical dominance, which not only explains why I
should do it but also why I should do it more religiously. To
that extent, this is a gardener's how-to book.

It's also a book for browsing. For discovering that a fairy
ring is a circle in the grass that marks the periphery of an
underground fungal growth, and that the name came from
the belief that such circles were a dancing ground for fairies.
I may never use this information, any more than I am likely
to make a ha-ha, but the next time I come across these
words, I'll know what they mean. More important, I'll know
where to look them up.

Similarly, I like knowing that Saint Fiacre, the patron saint of gardeners, is also the patron saint of Paris taxi drivers; that the correct way to pronounce the surname of the great Gertrude Jekyll is Gee′kill, and why gardeners to this day hold her in reverence. So this is also a book about garden history, great garden figures, and even great gardens and garden institutions. I think of it as a dictionary of horticultural literacy.

On a personal note, I am neither a botanist nor a horticulturist, but an enthusiastic amateur gardener and a professional garden-book editor. In both roles I constantly come across words and references that I need to look up. And despite my many shelves of garden books, I haven't found the single volume that holds the answers to questions that constantly arise. Obviously this one book can't do more than fulfill the needs that I personally recognize — readers will surely find their own omissions. I hope they aren't too numerous or too egregious. Moreover, since I am not an authority, Rita Buchanan, who is, was gracious enough to read and correct this manuscript. Any errors that may have slipped in are entirely my responsibility.

— *Frances Tenenbaum*

Abies
The botanical name for fir.

abortive
Imperfectly developed; especially, failing to produce seeds.

abscission
The controlled separation of flowers, leaves, and fruits from plants. It is the process that is at work when ripe fruit falls to the ground or the leaves fall off trees in autumn.

abscission zone
The layer of cells at the base of the leaf, flower, or fruit stem that, when it weakens, causes the organ's separation from the plant.

Abutilon
The botanical name for flowering maple and Chinese lantern.

acaulescent
Apparently stemless; actually, with a very short stem that may be below ground.

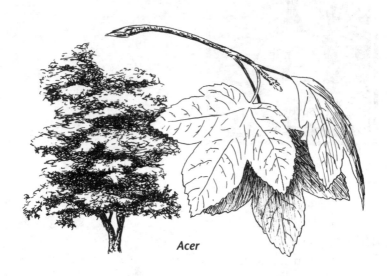

Acer

accelerator
A bacterial substance added to a compost pile to speed the decomposition of organic materials. Also called activator; compost activator.

accent plant
An individual plant that contrasts with its surroundings and catches your attention.

acclimatization
The physiological adaptation of a plant to changes in climate or site, such as in light, temperature, or altitude.

accrescent
Increasing in size with age.

-aceae
The Latin ending that indicates a plant family. For example, the Oriental poppy, *Papaver orientale,* belongs to the poppy family, Papaveraceae. Although Latin genus and species names are italicized, the family name (for some reason) is not.

Acer
The botanical name for maple.

achene
A dry one-seeded fruit that does not split. For example, what appear to be the seeds on the surface of a strawberry are actually the true fruits.

Achillea
The botanical name for yarrow.

acid rain
Rainwater that is acidic because it contains sulfur dioxide and other pollutants emitted from some industrial facilities. In parts of the United States and Canada, acid rain has damaged and even caused the death of forest trees many hundreds of miles from the source of the emissions.

acid soil
Soil with a pH lower than 7. Commonly found in high-rainfall regions. A pH of 6 is considered slightly acid, pH 5 is acid, and pH 4 is very acid. Many garden plants thrive in soil with a pH between 6 and 7. *See also* **pH**.

Achillea

Aconitum

Aconitum
The botanical name for monkshood.

Acorus
The botanical name for sweet flag.

Actaea
The botanical name for baneberry.

Acorus

actinomorphic
A term used to describe a
flower that is radially
symmetrical. Any cut through
the center divides it into two
equal parts. Two examples are
crocus and lily. *See also*
zygomorphic; regular flower.

actinomorphic

activator
See **accelerator.**

acute
Tapering to a point. Usually used to describe leaves.

Adiantum
The botanical name for maidenhair fern.

adpressed
Flatly pressed back, such as a leaf that lies flat against the
stem. For example, the tiny scalelike needles on the false

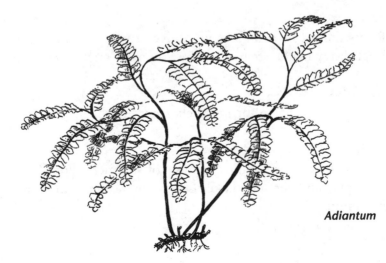
Adiantum

cypress, *Chamaecyparis,* are flattened against the stem — or adpressed — in fanlike sprays.

adventitious

Growing in an unexpected or unusual position, such as new shoots growing out of the trunks of trees or roots growing from the climbing stems of vines.

adventitious

adventive

An exotic plant that gets established briefly or locally but does not survive long or spread far.

aerate

To supply oxygen to the soil by digging or by turning it over. Earthworms improve aeration by tunneling through the soil. To aerate a lawn, a tool called an aerator, which has hollow tines, can be used to remove cores of sod and thatch.

aerial roots

Roots that grow from a stem, above ground level, as in English ivy or the stems of some epiphytic (air) plants.

Aesculus

The botanical name for horse chestnut and buckeye.

aestiv-

As part of a species name, means "of summer." For example, summer snowflake, *Leucojum aestivum,* blooms in summer.

air layering

Agapanthus
The botanical name for lily-of-the-Nile.

air layering
A method of propagating certain woody plants by making a cut in the stem and wrapping it in damp moss, then sealing the wrapped cut in plastic to keep it moist. New roots will form at the wound. In some cases, rooting may take as long as two or more years. *See also* **layering**.

Ajuga
The botanical name for bugleweed.

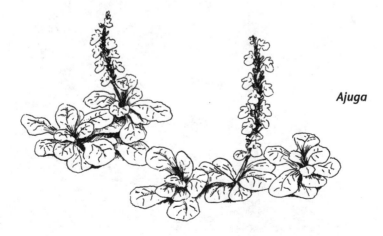

Ajuga

alatus, -a, -um

As a species name, means "having winged parts." For example, four thin woody "wings" or ridges run lengthwise along the stems of burning bush, *Euonymus alatus*.

alb-

As part of a species name, means "white." For example, gas plant, *Dictamnus albus*, has white flowers.

Alcea

The botanical name for hollyhock.

Alchemilla

The botanical name for lady's mantle.

alga (plural: algae)

A flowerless plant of extremely simple structure, usually green but in the seaweeds often beautifully colored. Algae range in size from the microscopic organisms that cover ponds with green scum to the giant kelp, a seaweed more than 100 feet long.

Alchemilla

alkaline soil
Soil with a pH higher than 7. Commonly found in low-rainfall regions. *See also* **pH**.

alkaloid
A plant compound containing nitrogen that, possibly because of its bitter taste, defends plants against predators. Alkaloids also include plant poisons or medicines. Nicotine, cocaine, and quinine are examples of plant alkaloids.

All-America Rose Selections, Inc. (AARS)
An association of rose producers and introducers that since 1938 has evaluated new rose hybrids to find the best for American gardeners. Winners are selected on completion of a two-year testing process, known as the AARS Trials, in 22 official test gardens throughout the United States.

All-America Selections (AAS)
An industry-based network of trial gardens that test new cultivars of vegetables and flowers and award prizes to those judged best. Some well-known gold medal winners are *Coreopsis* 'Early Sunrise', 'Sugar Snap' peas, and *Zinnia* 'Thumbelina'. All AAS winners can be raised from seed.

allée
A formal planting, usually of trees, lining both sides of a path or drive.

allelopathy
The release of chemicals by a plant to inhibit the growth of other plants in its immediate vicinity. Allelopathy is the reason why some plants, including tomatoes, will not grow near walnut trees.

Allium
The botanical name for ornamental onions.

Alnus
The botanical name for alder.

alpine
A small plant suitable for growing in a rock garden. Most alpines are native to mountain habitats.

alpine house
An unheated greenhouse specifically designed for alpine plants. Such structures are more common in Great Britain than in the United States.

Alstroemeria
The botanical name for Peruvian lily.

alternate
Occurring singly on alternate sides of a stem, not in pairs or whorls. Usually refers to leaves. *See also* **opposite**.

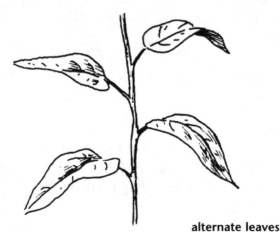

alternate leaves

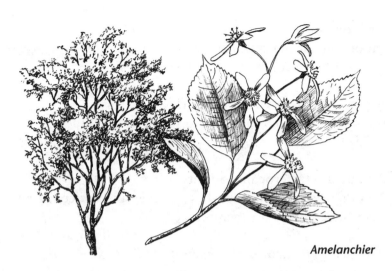

Amelanchier

alternate host
A plant upon which a plant disease lives for only part of its life cycle, depending upon some other, and usually unrelated, plant for completing it. Common examples are juniper or eastern red cedar and apple, which cohost cedar-apple rust. The remedy is to remove one of the hosts and so break the life cycle.

alternifolius, -a, -um
As a species name, means "with leaves arranged alternately," not in pairs or whorls. For example, most dogwoods have opposite leaves, but the pagoda dogwood, *Cornus alternifolia,* has alternate leaves.

amabilis, -e
As a species name, means "lovely." For example, beautybush, *Kolkwitzia amabilis,* has lovely pink flowers.

Amelanchier
The botanical name for shadbush, also known as serviceberry or Juneberry.

amendment
An organic or mineral material such as peat moss or perlite that is used to condition or improve the soil.

American Forestry Association
A society dedicated to balanced forest use, founded in 1875. It sponsors tree-planting and educational programs.

American Hemerocallis Society
An organization that publishes an extensive source list and has a slide library for members.

American Horticultural Society (AHS)
A nationwide organization of amateur gardeners and professional horticulturists, dedicated to promoting gardening. Based at River Farm in Alexandria, Virginia.

American Iris Society
An organization with 24 regional affiliates and 127 chapters. There are subsections devoted to different types of irises.

American Orchid Society
An organization with almost 30,000 members and more than 550 affiliated local societies. It is the major source of information about orchids for both scientific researchers and hobbyists.

American Rock Garden Society
An organization for avid rock gardeners, with many local chapters and a major annual conference.

Amsonia
The botanical name for bluestar.

Amsonia

anaerobe
An organism that can live without oxygen. Many fungi and bacteria are anaerobic.

Ananas
The botanical name for pineapple.

Anchusa
The botanical name for bugloss.

Andromeda
The botanical name for bog rosemary.

Anethum
The botanical name for dill.

angiosperms
The flowering plants, the largest group in the plant kingdom, with about 250,000 species. The name derives from the fact that the seeds are enclosed in an ovary. Angiosperms provide us with our flowers, the vegetables in our diet, and our hardwood trees. *See also* **gymnosperms**.

angustifolius, -a, -um
As a species name, means "narrow-leaved." For example, Russian olive, *Elaeagnus angustifolia,* has very slender gray leaves.

annual
1. A plant that germinates, grows, flowers, sets seed, and dies over a few months' time. Most annuals germinate in spring and die in late summer or fall, but they can grow at any time of the year if conditions are favorable.
2. A plant that is treated as an annual and grown for only one season's display. Many kinds of perennials, bulbs, grasses, and tropical plants are called annuals by gardeners. For example, impatiens and begonias are often used as annual bedding plants, but they are actually tropical perennials and would keep growing indefinitely if protected from frost.

annual ring
In a tree or shrub, the ring of wood developed during each growing season, as seen in a cross section of the trunk. When the trunk is cut, the rings can be counted to determine the age of the plant. Also called growth ring.

annual ring

annuus, -a, -um
As a species name, means "annual." For example, the common sunflower, *Helianthus annuus,* is an annual.

Anthemis
The botanical name for chamomile.

anther
The terminal part of a stamen, containing pollen in one or more pollen sacs.

anthesis
The opening of a flower ready for pollination.

anthracnose
A soilborne fungal disease that affects a wide variety of herbaceous and woody plants, causing leaf spots, leaf drop, wilting, and sometimes death.

Antirrhinum
The botanical name for snapdragon.

antitranspirant
A substance that is sprayed on the stems and leaves of plants to reduce the rate of transpiration, or water loss. Often used to protect evergreens from dry winter winds.

anvil pruning shears
Hand pruners that cut like a knife against a board; stronger than bypass pruners but more likely to damage the stem. *See also* **bypass pruning shears.**

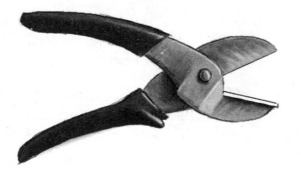

anvil
pruning
shears

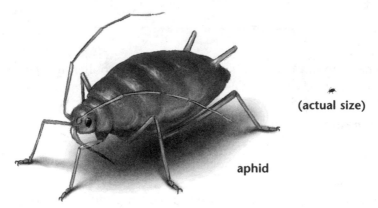

(actual size)

aphid

aphid
A small sucking insect that feeds primarily on new soft growth.

apical
Borne or arising from the growing tip of a stem.

apical bud
A bud at the tip of a stem.

apical dominance
The tendency of the central or terminal shoot that grows upward to inhibit the development of branching side shoots. To make a plant bushier or shorter, gardeners pinch the terminal shoots, which then permits the side shoots to develop.

apical meristem
A concentration of special cells at the tip of a stem, shoot, or root. When these cells divide and expand, the stem or root grows taller or longer. *See also* **primary growth.**

aquatic
A plant that grows submerged in water, although its roots are in soil. The most common aquatics are water lilies and lotus.

Aquilegia
The botanical name for columbine.

Arabis
The botanical name for rockcress.

Araucaria
The botanical name for Norfolk Island pine.

arbor
A shady resting place in a garden or park, often made of rustic materials or latticework on which plants such as climbing shrubs or vines are grown. Sometimes called a bower.

arborescent
Branching, like a tree.

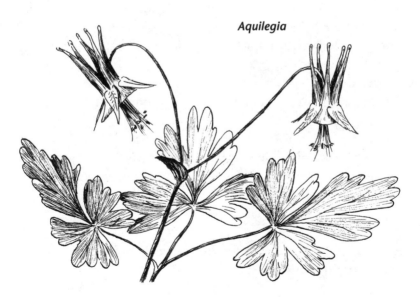

Aquilegia

Arctostaphylos

arboretum
Technically, a garden or collection of trees, often rare ones, grown for study, research, or ornament. In practice, most arboretums also display shrubs and other plants.

Arboretum at Flagstaff, The
A 200-acre Arizona arboretum that is the only facility of its type in the Rocky Mountains to be located above 6,000 feet. It is devoted primarily to propagating native plants.

arboriculture
The art of growing and cultivating ornamental trees.

arborist
One who specializes in the care and maintenance of trees, that is, in planting and pruning and in diagnosing and treating diseases.

arborizing
Pruning an overgrown shrub into a treelike specimen with one or two main trunks.

archegonium
The female reproductive organ of a fern or moss.

Arctostaphylos
The botanical name for bearberry (or kinnikinnick) and manzanita.

Arctotis
The botanical name for African daisy.

areole
The pit on a cactus stem or pad from which a flower or a spine develops.

argent-
As part of a species name, means "silvery." For example, buffalo berry, *Shepherdia argentea,* has silvery leaves.

aril
An extra, often colored, coat or appendage to a seed. It is the aril that provides the brilliant color of the fruits of bittersweet vine, yew, and euonymus.

Arisaema
The botanical name for jack-in-the-pulpit.

Arisaema

armyworm
A caterpillar that
chews on grass
blades, leaving bare
spots in the lawn.

armyworm

(actual size)

Arnold Arboretum
The oldest public arboretum in the United States,
established in 1872. An affiliate of Harvard University and
a part of the Boston park system, the 265-acre arboretum
has the largest, most diverse, and best-documented
collection of trees and shrubs in the country. Over the
years, it has collected specimens from all over the world
and introduced many of the cultivars gardeners prize today.

aroid
A plant in the Araceae family, which includes many tropical
plants such as anthuriums, calla lilies, philodendrons, and
spathiphyllums, plus jack-in-the-pulpit and skunk cabbage.
All have small flowers crowded into a spadix and
surrounded by a spathe.

Aronia
The botanical name for chokeberry.

Aruncus
The botanical name for goatsbeard.

Aronia

arvensis, -e

As a species name, means "found in cultivated fields" (as either a crop or a weed). For example, scouring rush, *Equisetum arvense,* is a troublesome perennial weed in sandy fields.

Asarum

The botanical name for wild ginger.

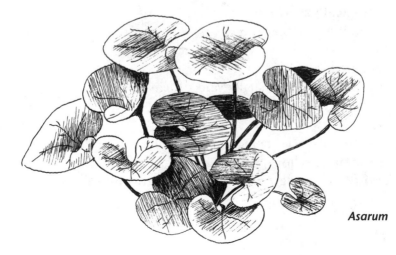

Asarum

Asclepias

Asclepias
The botanical name for milkweed.

asexual
As applied to propagation, indicates any method of increasing plants except by seeds, such as by cuttings, layering, or division.

Asteraceae
See Compositae.

astrological gardening
See moon gardening.

attenuated
Long and tapering. Usually said of leaves.

aureo-
As part of a species name, means "golden" or "yellow." For example, yellow-groove bamboo, *Phyllostachys aureosulcata,* has green stems with lengthwise yellow grooves.

auriculatus, -a, -um

As a species name, means "having ears or lobes." For example, *Coreopsis auriculata,* a perennial with daisylike yellow flowers, has leaves with one or two rounded lobes at the base.

auxin

A hormone that controls plant growth.

awn

A bristlelike appendage, especially on grass seeds.

awn

axil

The junction between a stem and a leaf. Each axil contains an axillary bud, which may develop into a new shoot.

axis

1. The central stalk of a compound leaf or flower cluster; the main stem of a plant. For example, the trunk is the axis of a pine tree.
2. An imaginary straight line that subdivides a garden, often marked by a walkway or path.

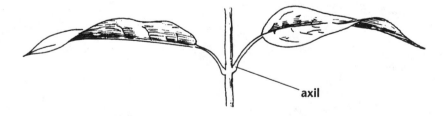

axil

Bacillus
A genus of biological insecticides that are generally
nontoxic (although they can harm some beneficial insects
such as butterfly larvae). Varieties of *Bacillus thuringiensis*
(also called Bt) control caterpillars, cabbage worms, and
mosquito larvae. *B. papilliae,* milky spore disease, controls
Japanese beetle grubs.

backbulb
On an orchid, an old pseudobulb that may be leafless but is
still alive and can be used for propagating a new plant.

backcross
A plant derived from a cross between a hybrid and one of
its parents.

backfill
Soil returned to a planting hole after the plant's roots have
been positioned. This can be original soil or soil with
amendments.

Bagatelle
The exuberantly rococo rose garden on the outskirts of
Paris, formally known as La Roseraie de Bagatelle. Since

1907, the garden has been the setting for the Concours International de Roses Nouvelle, popularly known as the Paris Rose Trials.

Bailey, Liberty Hyde (1858–1954)
The founder (1885) of the first college department of horticulture and landscape gardening in the United States, at Michigan State University. Bailey then joined Cornell University as professor of horticulture, later dean of the College of Agriculture. Published widely, he is today best known for *Hortus* (1930), a definitive reference work on plants in cultivation in the United States and Canada. *Hortus Third,* the most recent edition, was published in 1976 and prepared by the staff of the L. H. Bailey Hortorium of Cornell University.

balled-and-burlapped
Dug out of the ground with a ball of soil around the roots, which is wrapped in burlap and tied for transport.

Bambusa
The botanical name for bamboo.

B and B
The common abbreviation for balled-and-burlapped.

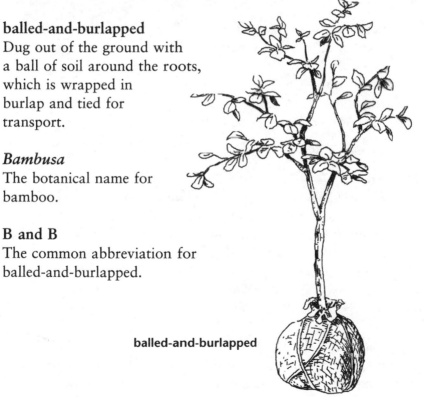

balled-and-burlapped

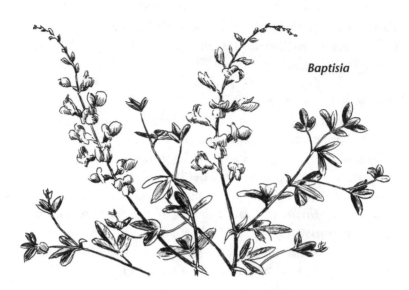

Baptisia

Baptisia
The botanical name for false indigo and wild indigo.

bare-root
Dug out of the ground when dormant, then shaken or washed to remove the soil from the roots before storage or shipment.

bark
The tough covering on the outside of woody trunks, stems, and roots, consisting of two layers: the outer bark, which is dead, and the inner bark, which contains living tissues (the cambium and phloem). Successive layers of bark are formed inside one another as the plant grows. The outer, older layers often crack apart or peel off when they cannot stretch any farther.

Bartram, John (1699–1777)
A Quaker farmer and botanist, one of the most famous explorers and plant collectors of his day. He established the

first botanical garden in the American colonies on his farm near Philadelphia. The house and garden have been restored and are open to the public. Only plants grown by Bartram or his son, William, were replanted.

basal break
A new shoot that emerges from the base of a severely pruned shrub.

basal leaf
A leaf that grows at the base of an herbaceous plant, often different in size and shape from leaves that grow on the upright flowering stems.

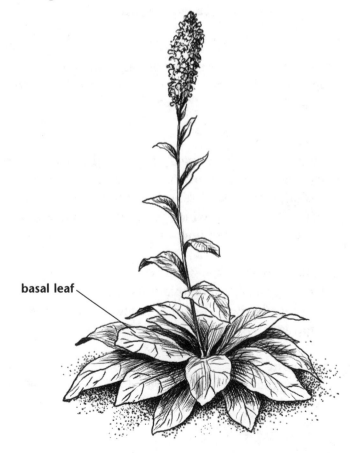

basal leaf

Bayard Cutting Arboretum

A 690-acre private estate, designed by Frederick Law Olmsted in 1887 and given to the Long Island (New York) Park Commission in 1952. Although the site suffered severe damage from Hurricane Gloria in 1985, the pinetum features many specimens that date back to the original plantings. The arboretum has the most extensive collections of firs, spruces, pines, hemlocks, cypress, and yews on Long Island.

beard

The hairs on the lower petals of some irises, from which the bearded iris derives its name. The awn on some grasses and cereals is also called a beard.

bed

A distinct, isolated flower or vegetable plot, visible from all sides, usually surrounded by lawn or walks. Also called island bed.

bedding out

Filling a bed with a mass of identical flowers to create an unchanging display of color or of designs. This rigid style was popular in Victorian days and is still seen in municipal plantings, some of which spell out the name of the town. *See also* **carpet bedding**.

bedding plant

A fast-growing annual plant used to create a mass display of colorful flowers or foliage. These are short-term plantings that must be replaced each season.

bee plant

A plant that yields considerable amounts of nectar and pollen to attract bees. Bee plants include clovers, milkweeds, salvias, linden trees, wisteria vines, and fruit trees, especially apple trees.

Belamcanda
The botanical name for blackberry lily.

Belgian fence
A style of espalier in which limbs are trained into a latticelike pattern.

bell jar
From the Victorian era, a glass, bell-shaped jar with a knob at the top, used to protect a delicate plant from dry wind, cold, and heavy rain. A modern version is the cloche.

beneficial insect
Any insect that improves the soil, pollinates plants, or controls harmful pests. Beneficial insects include earthworms, bees, ladybugs, and lacewing larvae.

Belgian fence

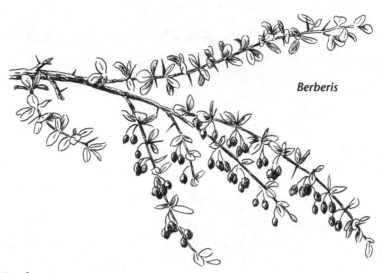

Berberis

Berberis
The botanical name for barberry.

berm
A mound, small hill, or ridge of earth intended to provide screening or to direct water runoff. On small properties and especially in front gardens, a planted berm helps to create privacy.

Bernheim Forest Arboretum
A large forest, nature center, and garden in Clermont, Kentucky. The arboretum contains almost 2,000 labeled specimens of trees and shrubs.

berry
A fleshy fruit with one to many seeds that is developed from a single ovary.

Berry Botanic Garden
A small garden in Portland, Oregon, that features a very special collection of rhododendrons, lilies, primroses, and other plants that grow well in the Pacific Northwest.

Betula
The botanical name for birch.

biennial
A plant that requires two years to complete its life cycle. During the first growing season, the seed germinates and the plant grows but produces only foliage. During the second growing season, it flowers, sets seed, and dies. If allowed to reseed themselves, biennials can keep the garden in flowers indefinitely. Two popular biennials are foxglove (*Digitalis purpurea*) and, despite its species name, money plant (*Lunaria annua*).

biennis, -e
As a species name, means "biennial," like the common evening primrose, *Oenothera biennis*.

bifurcate
Forked or divided into two branches like the letter Y.

Betula

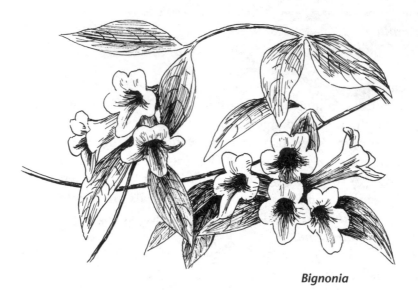

Bignonia

Bignonia
The botanical name for trumpet vine.

Biltmore House and Gardens
In Asheville, North Carolina, the former Vanderbilt mansion modeled after the great châteaux of France. The formal gardens are based on those of Vaux-le-Vicomte, and the 250-acre landscape is one of the best-preserved designs of Frederick Law Olmsted.

binomial
A "two-name name," the two words in Latin that make up the botanical or scientific names of plants. The first word identifies the genus, the second the species. *See also* **Linnaeus, Carolus; botanical Latin.**

biological control
A system of controlling plant pests and diseases without the use of chemicals, by employing predators and parasites that

feed upon them. For example, populations of ladybugs can be introduced into the garden to consume aphids.

biota
The combined flora and fauna of a region.

Birmingham Botanical Garden
A municipally owned facility established in 1962 that includes a variety of special gardens. The wildflower garden in a former rock quarry features Alabama wildflowers. The Japanese garden is accented by the teahouse originally built for the 1965 New York World's Fair.

bisexual
In botany, having both stamens and pistils in the same flower. Such flowers are also called perfect.

black spot
A fungal disease of roses that shows up as black spots on the leaves. Oddly enough, the fungus seems to thrive in clean air; city roses are rarely infected.

blade
The broad flat part of a leaf.

blade

bleeding

Said of plants like milkweed or poppy that exude sap when cut. Many trees, such as pines, birches, and maples, bleed sap if pruned at the wrong season.

Blithewold Gardens and Arboretum

A turn-of-the-century summer residence in Bristol, Rhode Island, with gardens typical of the time. Many of the arboretum's trees date back to 1900, when the garden was planted. They include an 80-foot giant sequoia, the largest specimen east of the Rocky Mountains.

bloom

1. A flower.
2. A whitish powdery or waxy covering on some fruits or plant parts.

blossom end rot

A cultural problem caused by a calcium deficiency. It is often related to temperature extremes, uneven watering, or root damage. Plants affected include tomatoes and peppers.

bog

An area of soft, naturally waterlogged land characterized by extreme acidity.

bog garden

A landscaped natural or artificial bog.

bole

The trunk of a tree below the lowest branch.

bolting

The rapid growth of a stem prior to flowering. Usually refers to annuals or biennials that have been stressed by heat, cold, drought, crowding, or transplanting.

bonemeal
A natural high-phosphorus fertilizer made from crushed and powdered animal bones. It works more slowly than the chemical fertilizer superphosphate. Like the latter, it is often used at planting time because phosphate stimulates root growth.

bones
In the language of garden design, the permanent structural elements that give shape to the garden—the skeleton. These elements include paths, walls, steps, fences, trellises, hedges, and other elements that provide the framework for the plants.

bonsai
The Japanese art of pruning and shaping trees and shrubs that produces long-lived miniature container plants.

bonsai

Borago

Borago
The botanical name for borage.

border
Usually, a long narrow garden bed, backed by shrubs,
buildings, walls, fences, or other defining backgrounds.
A herbaceous border is composed primarily of perennials,
bulbs, and annuals. A mixed border also includes shrubs
and possibly trees.

borer
Any of various grubs or larvae of many beetles or sawflies
that eat the heartwood or, more often, the cambium of
many trees.

botanical
A natural insecticide, such as pyrethrin, rotenone, and
sabadilla. Although these are naturally occurring
substances, they are also poisons that can harm mammals,
birds, and fish.

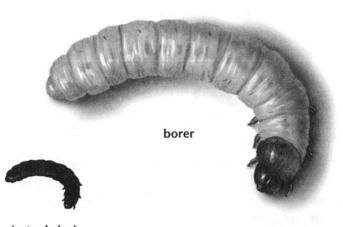

borer

(actual size)

botanical Latin

The language used to denote the scientific names of plants. In the 18th century, when Carolus Linnaeus invented the binomial system for plant classification, Latin was the universal language of scientists. In his system (still in use today) the first Latin word indicated the genus and the second pinpointed the species. Since that time, many new names for plants have been derived from other languages, especially Greek, or from the name of the place where a previously unknown plant was first found or the person who discovered or cultivated it. Whatever their origin, however, all scientific plant names are treated as Latin. Thus the redbud tree is *Cercis* (from the Greek) *canadensis* (from the place where it was first identified). The Siberian wallflower is *Cheiranthus* (from the Greek) *allionii* (after the Italian botanist Carlo Allioni). *See also* **Linnaeus, Carolus; binomial.**

botanic garden

Also called botanical garden. Primarily an institution for research in the field of botany and, by extension,

bract

horticulture. The modern botanic garden will have, besides research laboratories, a library and herbarium; large collections of growing plants, both outdoors and in a greenhouse; and usually elaborate gardens.

botanize
To collect plants for study.

botany
The science or study of plants.

botrytis
A fungus that attacks lettuce, strawberries, and many other plants, forming soft scummy patches of gray mold. Also called gray mold.

bottle garden
See terrarium.

bottom heat
Heat applied to the bottom of propagating beds or flats to speed or aid in the germination of seeds or the rooting of cuttings.

bottom watering
Setting a pot in a shallow tray of water and leaving it there long enough to wet the soil from the bottom up. Often

recommended for pots of seeds or seedlings, to avoid splashing them out of place.

bough
A branch of a tree, especially a large one.

bower
See **arbor**.

Boyce Thompson Southwestern Arboretum
Located in Superior, Arizona, an arboretum featuring plantings of cacti and succulents, and dramatic spurts of flowers following spring rains.

bract
A special modified leaf located at the base of a flower or inflorescence. Bracts may be small or large, green or colored. On some plants, such as poinsettias, dogwoods, and bromeliads, what appear to be flower petals are actually colorful bracts.

bramble
Blackberry, raspberry, and related shrubs. All have prickly or thorny stems.

branch
A secondary woody stem or limb growing from the trunk or main stem of a plant.

branch collar
The swelling where a branch joins the trunk of a tree.

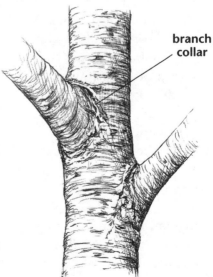

branch collar

Brassica
The botanical name for vegetables in the cabbage family (Cruciferae, formerly Brassicaceae), including cauliflower, Brussels sprouts, broccoli, and, of course, cabbages.

broadcast
To distribute seeds or fertilizer evenly over an area, not in rows.

broad-leaved evergreen
An evergreen tree or shrub that is not a conifer.

bromeliad
An epiphytic plant of the family Bromeliaceae, or pineapple family.

Brooklyn Botanic Garden
An institution established in 1910 by a group of private citizens (on the site of a former city dump) in Brooklyn, New York. The BBG was a pioneer in horticultural education, a role it continues to play today. Among its most important features are the rose garden, the Japanese garden, the fragrance garden for the blind, and three new glasshouses featuring collections of tropical, desert, and temperate-region plants. It also publishes a series of handbooks on various aspects of gardening.

Brookside Gardens
A 50-acre botanic garden in Wheaton, Maryland, with excellent displays of hardy ornamental shrubs, perennials, roses, and wildflowers.

Brown, Lancelot "Capability" (1716–1783)
One of England's most famous garden designers. He got his nickname from his conviction that all gardens had

"capabilities" within them (awaiting his redesign). Before him, most English estate gardens were laid out in geometrical symmetry. Brown, applying the principles of "naturalism," emphasized asymmetry, using serpentine curves and trees planted in loosely scattered groups. His gardens gave the estates a parklike look.

Bt
The common abbreviation for *Bacillus thuringiensis. See also* **Bacillus**.

bud
A young and undeveloped leaf, flower, or shoot, usually covered tightly with scales.

Buddleia
The botanical name for butterfly bush.

Buddleia

bud union
See graft union.

builder's sand
See sharp sand.

bulb

A storage organ, usually
formed underground. The
swollen portion consists
mostly of fleshy, food-storing
scales attached to a short
flat stem. Onions, for
example, are bulbs.

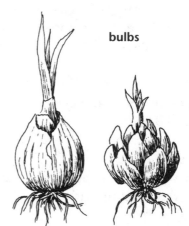

bulbs

bulbil

A small bulblike structure, usually borne among the flowers
or in the axil of a leaf but never at ground level like a true
bulb.

bulblet

A small bulb produced at the base of a larger bulb.

bunchgrass

A grass that forms compact clumps and does not spread by
stolons or rhizomes. Desirable ornamental grasses are often
bunchgrasses. Also called clumping grass.

bur

A rough or prickly husk or covering of a seed or fruit, as in
the chestnut or burdock.

bush

A many-branched small shrub with no distinct main stem
or stems.

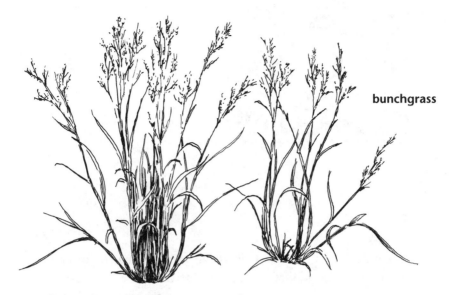

bunchgrass

butterfly garden

A garden featuring plants that attract butterflies and their larvae.

Buxus

The botanical name for boxwood.

bypass pruning shears

Pruners that cut with a scissorlike motion. *See also* **anvil pruning shears**.

bypass pruning shears

cactus

A plant in the immense Cactaceae family. The majority are spiny succulent plants. Most are native to the dry desert regions of the Americas, but a few are tropical epiphytes.

caeruleus, -a, -um

As a species name, means "dark blue." For example, Jacob's ladder, *Polemonium caeruleum,* has blue flowers.

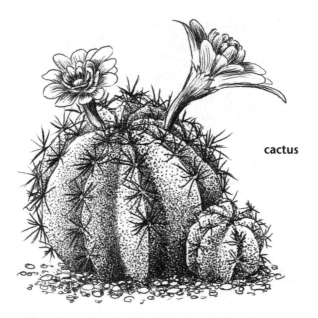

cactus

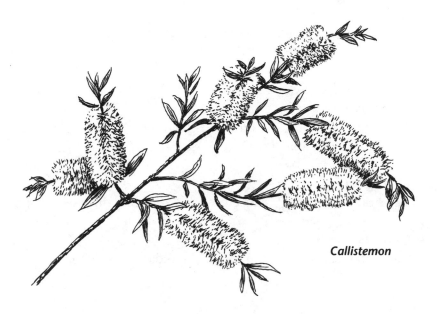

Callistemon

caliche
A hard deposit of white limestone that sometimes underlies alkaline soils in arid climates.

Callaway Gardens
A vast, beautifully landscaped park in Pine Mountain, Georgia, with outstanding collections of native and exotic azaleas, hollies, and magnolias, plus seasonal displays and greenhouses, including a special greenhouse designed as a butterfly garden, complete with countless live butterflies.

Callicarpa
The botanical name for beautyberry.

Callistemon
The botanical name for bottlebrush.

Calluna
The botanical name for heather.

callus
1. The corklike tissue that is developed to cover wounds in the bark of a tree or shrub.
2. A zone of rapidly dividing cells at the base of a cutting that precedes root formation.

Calochortus
The botanical name for mariposa lily and star tulip.

Caltha
The botanical name for marsh marigold.

calyx
Collectively, the sepals of a flower.

cambium
A layer of cells that divide to produce new tissue in plant stems. Actually, there are two kinds of cambium. The vascular cambium makes possible the thickening or increase in girth of a plant stem. It gives off new cells in two directions, making xylem toward the inside of the stem and phloem toward the outside. The cork cambium produces the outer bark that protects woody stems and roots. *See also* **secondary growth**.

Campanula
The botanical name for bellflower.

campestris, -e
As a species name, means "growing in or associated with fields." For example, the hedge maple, *Acer campestre,* was

traditionally planted for hedgerows around pastures and fields.

Campsis
The botanical name for trumpet creeper.

canadensis, -e
As a species name, means "native to Canada" but was used by early botanists for plants that range down into the eastern United States. For example, columbine, *Aquilegia canadensis,* grows wild from Canada to as far south as Florida and Texas.

Canadian Wildflower Society
A society devoted exclusively to the wild flora of North America. It publishes a handsome magazine.

candidus, -a, -um
As a species name, means "pure, shining white." For example, the Madonna lily, *Lilium candidum,* has glossy white flowers.

candle pruning
A technique for pruning pines and other conifers by snapping off the new shoots, or "candles," after they elongate but before they harden. This produces a more compact but natural-looking specimen.

candle pruning

cane
A long, woody, pliable stem, as of grapevines or climbing roses.

canker
A sunken area, sometimes soft or rotten, on woody stems or twigs. It can be caused by several kinds of fungi or bacteria.

canopy
The uppermost layer in a woods or a forest, formed by the crowns of the trees.

Cape Cod weeder
A hand-weeding tool with a narrow L-shaped blade, useful for weeding in tight areas.

capillary water
Moisture held in the tiny spaces between soil particles. It is the principal source of moisture for a plant's roots.

capitate
Forming a dense compact head of flowers, as in the alliums.

capsule
A dry seedpod that splits open when ripe.

Cape Cod weeder

Carex
The botanical name for sedge.

carnivorous plant
A plant that captures insects and digests them to get the nitrogen that is in short supply in the marshes where most of these plants grow. Among the best-known carnivorous plants (also called insectivorous plants) are the Venus flytrap (*Dionaea muscipula*), pitcher plants (*Sarracenia* spp.), and the various sundews (*Drosera* spp.).

carolinianus, -a, -um
As a species name, means "native to the Carolinas" but was used by early botanists for plants that grow throughout the eastern United States. For example, the hornbeam or musclewood tree, *Carpinus caroliniana*, grows from Minnesota and Massachusetts to Texas and Florida.

carpel
The female reproductive organs of a flower, containing an ovary, stigma, and style. The pistil can contain one or more carpels.

carpet bedding
A mass planting of low, mostly foliage plants in patterns that resemble the designs in Oriental carpets. It was a popular style of planting in Victorian public gardens but is rarely seen today. *See also* **bedding out.**

Carpinus
The botanical name for hornbeam.

-carpus, -a, -um
As part of a species name, refers to the fruits. For example, black chokeberry, *Aronia melanocarpa*, bears dark blue-black berries.

Caryopteris
The botanical name for blue spirea, or bluebeard.

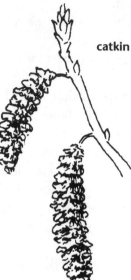

catkin

catkin
A dense spike of small, petalless, often unisexual flowers, most often found on wind-pollinated trees or shrubs.

Cattleya
The botanical name for any of several related genera of orchids that make up the Cattleya Alliance.

caulescent
Having an obvious stem, usually above ground.

cauline
Of, having, or growing on a stem. Used especially to describe leaves arising from the upper part of a stem.

-caulis, -e
As part of a species name, refers to the stem. For example, the pink lady's slipper orchid, *Cypripedium acaule,* appears to be stemless (actually the stem is underground).

cedar-apple rust
A fungal disease affecting junipers, apples, and crab apples. *See also* alternate host.

Cedrus
The botanical name for cedar.

Celastrus
The botanical name for bittersweet.

Cedrus

cell
The basic structural unit of an organism.

cell pack
A seedling container, usually of plastic, that consists of individual "cells" linked together. Commonly half a dozen such cells are joined in what is known as a six-pack. Unlike seedling flats, cell packs keep the roots of each seedling separate from those of adjacent seedlings.

cellulose
The main constituent of the cell walls in most plants.

Celtis
The botanical name for hackberry.

Centaurea
The botanical name for cornflower, mountain bluet, or bachelor's button.

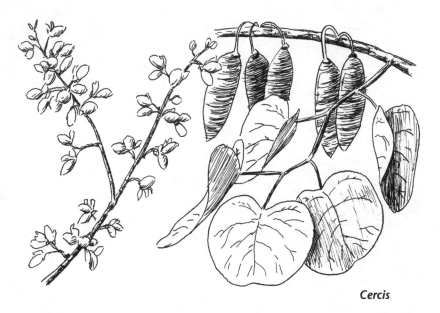

Cercis

Centranthus
The botanical name for valerian.

centripetal
Developing or progressing inward toward the center or axis, as in the head of a sunflower in which the oldest flowers are near the edge and the youngest flowers are in the center.

Cercidium
The botanical name for palo verde.

Cercis
The botanical name for redbud tree.

Chaenomeles
The botanical name for flowering quince.

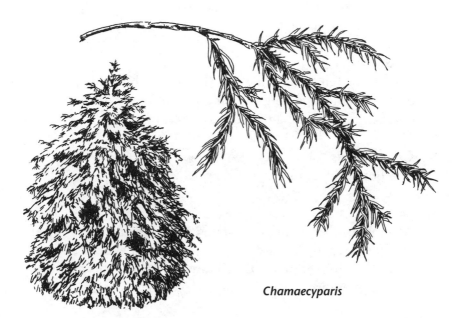

Chamaecyparis

chaff
1. The thin dry bracts or scales borne among the small individual flowers in the composite, or daisy, family.
2. The dry bracts enclosing mature grains of wheat and some other cereal plants, removed during threshing.

Chamaecyparis
The botanical name for false cypress.

chaparral
A dense growth of mostly small-leaved evergreen shrubs, as found in the foothills of California. Because the leaves are rich in highly flammable resins and because these shrubs normally grow on steep slopes, these areas are subject to frequent wildfires.

Chasmanthium
The botanical name for sea oats or spangle grass.

Cheekwood
Site of the Tennessee Botanical Garden, in Nashville, a 55-acre estate including formal and informal gardens, wildflower displays, and greenhouses.

Cheiranthus
The botanical name for wallflower.

chelate
A complex chemical that contains iron or some other metal in a form readily available to plants. Chelates are used by gardeners to treat plants that show the chlorosis typically caused by an iron or magnesium deficiency.

Chelone
The botanical name for turtlehead.

Chelone

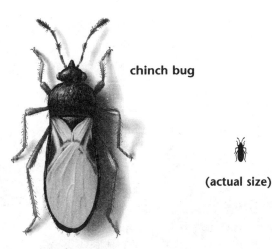

chinch bug

(actual size)

Chelsea Flower Show
England's annual extravaganza. If not the world's largest flower show, it is certainly the most famous. Held each spring in London.

chemical fertilizer
See inorganic fertilizer.

Chicago Botanic Garden
A 300-acre garden in Lisle, Illinois, built on a floodplain that is now a landscape of islands, lakes, and waterways. It features six different prairie types with appropriate plantings and a collection of native trees of Illinois.

chinch bug
A destructive insect whose larvae, smaller than a pinhead, suck the sap from grasses.

chinensis, -e
As a species name, means "native to China." Many cultivars of astilbe, for example, have been developed from the Chinese species, *Astilbe chinensis.*

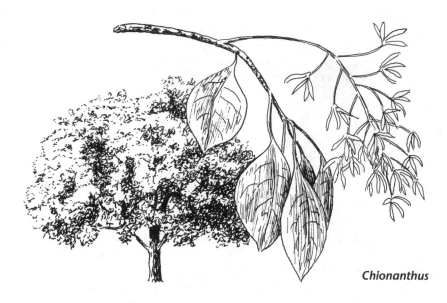

Chionanthus

Chionanthus
The botanical name for fringe tree.

Chionodoxa
The botanical name for glory-of-the-snow.

chipper
A machine for chopping brush and limbs into small chips that can be composted or used as mulch. *See also* **shredder**.

chloroblast
The cellular body containing chlorophyll and thus the place in which photosynthesis occurs.

chlorophyll
The green pigment in plant leaves that captures light and uses its energy to manufacture food in the process called photosynthesis.

chlorosis
A failure to produce the normal green coloring matter in leaves, causing them to become pale or yellowish. Usually caused by insufficient nitrogen or by a deficiency of iron or magnesium.

chrys-
As part of a species name, means "golden." For example, the western columbine, *Aquilegia chrysantha,* has golden yellow flowers.

Chrysogonum
The botanical name for green-and-gold.

Church, Thomas D. (1902–1978)
A California landscape designer known for the innovative gardens he designed for homes on steep hillsides. He used raised beds, wide wooden decks, and broad paved areas to create outdoor "rooms." His book *Gardens Are for People* propounded his view that gardens are an extension of the house and a place for people to entertain and to relax. He also advocated using native plants that would be easy to maintain.

cilium (plural: cilia)
One of the hairs along the margin or edge of a structure, such as a leaf, usually forming a fringe.

Cimicifuga
The botanical name for black snakeroot, black cohosh, or bugbane.

cinereus, -a, -um
As a species name, means "ash-colored" or "gray." For example, dusty miller, *Senecio cineraria,* has silver-gray leaves.

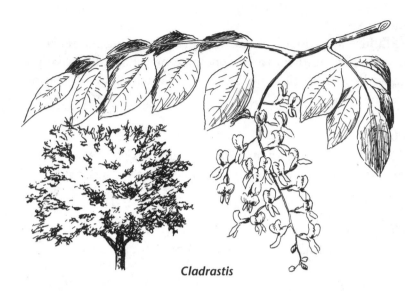

Cladrastis

Cistus
The botanical name for rock rose.

citriodorus, -a, -um
As a species name, means "lemon scented." For example, the lemon gum, *Eucalyptus citriodora,* has lemon-scented leaves.

cladode
A flattened stem that performs the function of a leaf; an example is the pad of the opuntia cactus.

Cladrastis
The botanical name for yellowwood.

clasping
Surrounding or partly surrounding the stem, as in the base of the leaves of certain plants, such as tulips.

claw
A narrow place at the base of a petal, found in some kinds of irises, roses, pinks, and other flowers. Such petals are said to be clawed.

clay soil
Soil composed of extremely small particles, with a large capacity for holding water and dissolved plant nutrients. Unamended clay soil is sticky, heavy, and hard to work. It tends to expand when wet and crack apart when dry.

Claytonia
The botanical name for spring beauty.

cleistogamous
A term that refers to the development of seed from an unopened, self-pollinated flower. Some violets, for example, are insect-pollinated in spring but develop cleistogamous buds in summer.

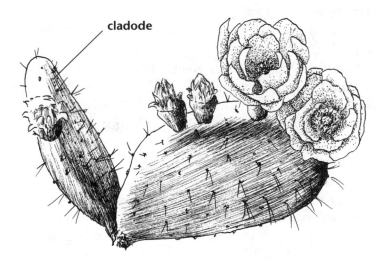

cladode

Clethra

Clethra
The botanical name for sweet pepperbush or summer-
sweet.

climate zones
A series of zones that represent different climatic conditions
in the United States and Canada, devised by horticulturists
for rating the hardiness of plants. Three systems are in
common usage today, and a few other systems have their
own advocates. A system originally developed at the
Arnold Arboretum in Boston and subsequently revised and
updated by the United States Department of Agriculture
designates 11 hardiness zones, based on average low
temperatures in winter.

Gardeners in the South are as interested in heat
tolerance as in cold hardiness and prefer a system used by
Southern Living magazine, which divides the region into
four zones — Upper South, Middle South, Lower South,
and Coastal Zone — and rates plants according to their
survival in these zones.

Gardeners from the Rocky Mountains west to the Pacific prefer a system developed by the publishers of *Sunset* magazine and the *Sunset Western Garden Book,* which divides the region into 24 climate zones, based on several factors of climate and topography, and rates plants accordingly. *See also* **hardiness zones.**

climax
The final natural stage of vegetation on a particular site. In the Northeast, for example, the climax vegetation would be a forest. In the Midwest, it might be a prairie. By definition, no garden could be a climax landscape because humans have added and subtracted plants and managed their growth.

climber
A plant that uses tendrils, twining stems, adhesive rootlets, or other means to extend itself up and over such supports as fences, trellises, or other plants.

cloche
A glass or rigid plastic cover used to protect plants from frost, wind, or rain. Originally, this French word for "dish cover" referred to the Victorian bell jar. Today it may indicate a cover for a single plant or for many.

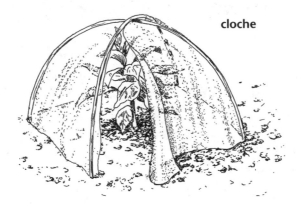

cloche

Cloisters, The

A branch of New York's Metropolitan Museum of Art devoted to medieval art, architecture, and gardens. The plants are those grown in western Europe during the Middle Ages. One of the gardens features the plants depicted in the famous Unicorn Tapestries.

clone

A group of genetically identical plants all produced by vegetative propagation from a single parent.

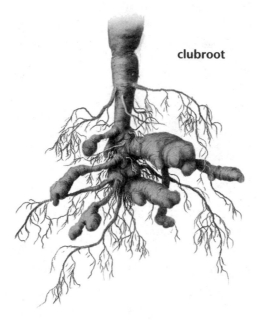

clubroot

clubroot

A disease affecting members of the cabbage family (Cruciferae), caused by a fungus that lives in the soil and produces large knots on the roots. Infected plants are stunted.

clumping grass

See bunchgrass.

cold frame

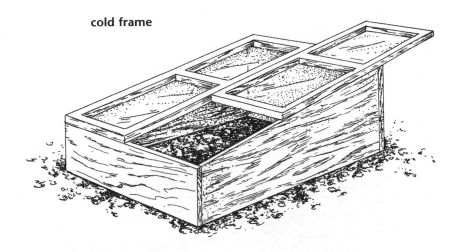

coccineus, -a, -um
As a species name, means "scarlet." For example, the wild red mallow, *Hibiscus coccineus,* has large, bright red flowers.

codling moth
An insect whose larva feeds inside developing apples.

cold compost
Compost made by allowing organic matter to decompose naturally at air temperature, over a period of months or years. Cold compost is easy to produce, but it typically contains seeds of weeds or garden plants that germinate when the compost is worked into the soil or spread as a mulch, and it may also harbor disease organisms. *See also* **hot compost; compost.**

cold frame
A low, bottomless, boxlike structure like a miniature greenhouse, used to shelter small plants. A clear glass or plastic top can be opened for ventilation.

collar

cold-hardiness
See **hardiness.**

collar
A bottomless band placed around the stem of a newly
planted tomato or other plant to protect against damage
from cutworms.

column
The fused structure formed by the union of stamens and
pistils in an orchid flower, or by the stamens in the flowers
of the mallow family (Malvaceae).

compactus, -a, -um
As a species name, or more commonly a variety or cultivar
name, means "growing smaller than average," with a
dense, compact habit. For example, dwarf inkberry holly,
Ilex glabra 'Compacta', grows only 4 to 6 feet tall, whereas
regular inkberry holly grows to 8 feet or taller.

companion planting

Growing certain plants, singly or together, in the hope of repelling insects or as deterrents to disease. For example, marigolds in the vegetable garden are said to repel nematodes.

complete fertilizer

A fertilizer that supplies nitrogen, phosphorus, and potassium, the three elements required in greatest quantities by plants. Note that a "complete" fertilizer does not necessarily supply the secondary and trace elements that are also required for healthy plant growth. *See also* **macronutrients; micronutrients; NPK.**

complete flower

A flower that has all of the normal flower parts, namely, the sepals, petals, stamens, and pistil.

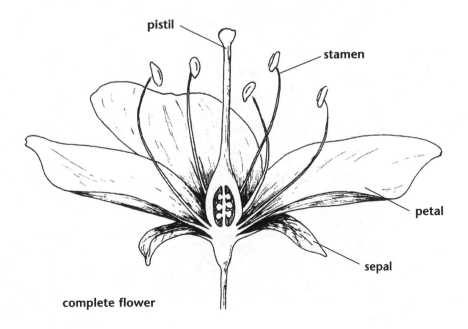

complete flower

Compositae
The composite or daisy family, whose members include daisies, asters, yarrows, dahlias, chrysanthemums, artemisias, and more than 100 other genera of ornamental plants. Also called Asteraceae.

composite
A plant in the family Compositae, whose members have many small flowers packed tightly together into inflorescences that resemble single blossoms.

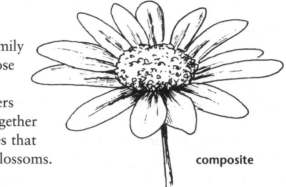

composite

compost
Decomposed organic matter, often referred to as "brown gold," that has the crumbly texture and feel of good garden soil. It is both a fertilizer and a soil conditioner. Materials suitable for a compost pile include

compost bin

leaves, grass clippings, dead plants, and vegetable kitchen wastes, as well as cow and horse manures. *See also* **cold compost; hot compost.**

compost activator
See **accelerator.**

compost bin
Any container bought or built to contain the ingredients of a compost pile.

compost tea
A solution made by soaking compost in water. The resulting "tea" is used as a liquid fertilizer. *See also* **manure tea.**

compound leaf
A leaf with two or more leaflets branching off a single petiole (stalk). *See also* **simple leaf.**

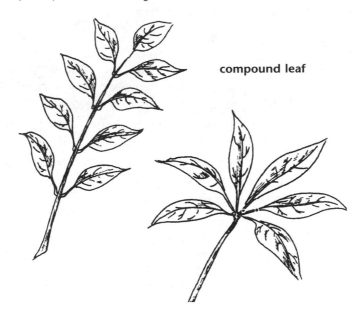

compound leaf

Comptonia

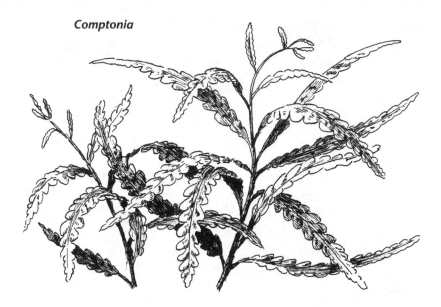

Comptonia
The botanical name for sweet fern.

conifer
A tree or shrub, often evergreen, usually with needlelike leaves, such as pine, spruce, or hemlock. A few conifers, including bald cypress, larch, and dawn redwood, have needlelike leaves but are deciduous. Another exception is the ginkgo, which has deciduous leaves that are fan shaped, not needlelike. Most conifers bear seeds in woody cones, but junipers, yews, plum yews, and ginkgoes have seeds with fleshy coats. *See also* **gymnosperms**.

coniferous
Of or relating to conifers.

conservatory
A greenhouse, especially one in which the plants are displayed aesthetically, as in a botanic garden. Also, a room for both plants and people.

Consolida
The botanical name for larkspur.

contact insecticide
A chemical that kills insects through skin contact; it does not have to be ingested. Insecticidal soap and horticultural oil are both contact insecticides. They must be sprayed directly on the insects to be effective; any insects that evade the spray survive. *See also* **systemic insecticide**.

container gardening
Growing a garden of outdoor plants in containers, typically on a rooftop or a small city plot.

container-grown
Raised in a pot that is removed before planting.

container-grown

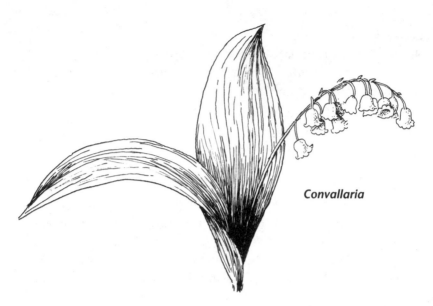

Convallaria

container plant
A plant that is, or usually is, grown in a pot for its entire lifetime. Indoor plants are almost always container plants.

contorted
Twisted spirally, as in the twisted Hankow willow, *Salix matsudana* 'Tortuosa'.

controlled-release fertilizer
A synthetic fertilizer, usually encased in gelatin capsules, that releases its nutrients over a specific period of time, much the same as a controlled-release drug releases its medicine. Also called timed-release fertilizer. *See also* **slow-release fertilizer**.

Convallaria
The botanical name for lily-of-the-valley.

Convolvulus
The botanical name for bindweed.

cool-season grass

A grass that grows most vigorously at temperatures below 60 to 70 degrees F and goes dormant and turns brown in hot weather. Cool-season lawn grasses include Kentucky bluegrass, perennial ryegrass, and the fescues. Cool-season ornamental grasses include blue fescue grass and feather reed grass. *See also* **warm-season grass.**

coppice

A thicket or grove of small trees or shrubs, especially one maintained by periodic cutting or pruning to encourage suckering, as in the cultivation of willow trees for basketry.

cordatus, -a, -um

As a species name, means "heart shaped." For example, the littleleaf linden, *Tilia cordata,* has heart-shaped leaves.

cordon

A tree or shrub, especially a fruit tree such as an apple or a pear, repeatedly pruned and trained to grow on a support as a single ropelike stem.

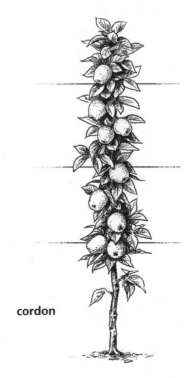

cordon

cork

The nonliving, water-resistant outer tissue of bark.

cork cambium

A layer of cells in the stem of woody plants that produces the outer bark. *See also* **cambium.**

corm

A solid, bulblike underground stem, resembling a bulb but without its scales and sometimes with a membranous coat. Typical examples are the corms of crocus and gladiolus. Corms bear roots at the base and nourish the young plant just as bulbs do.

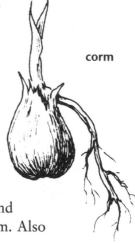

corm

cormel

A small corm that is produced by and develops alongside of its parent corm. Also called a cormlet.

Cornell mix

The original formula for soilless potting mixtures, developed at Cornell University. It includes peat moss, vermiculite, and nutrients. *See also* **soilless mix**.

Cornus

Cornus

The botanical name for dogwood trees and shrubs and for the ground cover bunchberry.

corolla

Collectively, the petals of a flower.

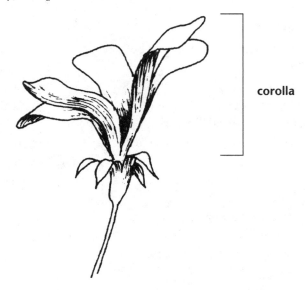

corolla

corona

A crownlike structure on some corollas, as in daffodils and the milkweed family (Asclepiadaceae).

Cortaderia

The botanical name for pampas grass.

cortex

In herbaceous plants, the layer of cells in the roots and stems immediately inside the epidermis, or "skin."

Corylopsis

The botanical name for winter hazel.

Corylus
The botanical name for filbert.

corymb
A flat-topped cluster of flowers, which begin blooming at the edge and proceed toward the center.

Cotinus
The botanical name for smoke tree.

cottage garden
A loose term generally referring to a front yard filled with informally planted flowers. A typical cottage garden has a front gate, a straight path leading to the door, and a romantic jumble of colorful old-fashioned flowers.

cotyledon
A food-storage organ in seeds. Monocot seeds have one cotyledon; dicot seeds have two. Also called seed leaf. *See also* **monocotyledon; dicotyledon.**

cover crop
A quick-growing crop used to cover exposed ground, prevent erosion, and retard leaching. *See also* **green manure.**

Crataegus
The botanical name for hawthorn.

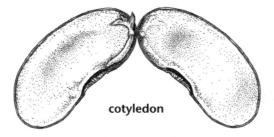

cotyledon

creeper
(Vinca)

creeper
A prostrate or trailing plant.

crenulate
Minutely scalloped.

crispus, -a, -um
As a species name, means "a crisp curly edge or texture,"
like the leaves of curly parsley, *Petroselinum crispum*.

Crockett, James Underwood (1915–1979)
The author of many practical gardening books and the
original host of the PBS-TV show *The Victory Garden*.

crop rotation
The planting of different species in rotation on the same
piece of land, to reduce the risk of soilborne diseases and
to vary the pattern of nutrient uptake.

cross-pollination
The transfer of pollen from a flower on one plant to a
flower on a different plant. Some species require cross-
pollination in order to set seed. *See also* **self-pollination**.

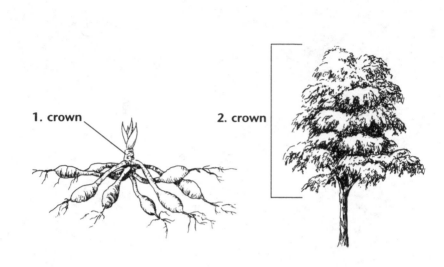

1. crown   2. crown

crotch
The point where a main branch of a tree joins the trunk.
See also **fork**.

crown
1. That part of a plant where the roots and stem meet,
   usually at soil level.
2. The part of a tree or shrub above the level of the lowest
   branch.

crown gall
A bacterial disease that
infects, weakens, and kills
many types of plants. The
brown, rough, woody galls,
often resembling blackened
walnuts, may be present on
larger roots near the surface
of the soil, as well as on the
crown. *See also* **gall**.

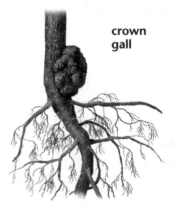

crown
gall

crucifer
A plant in the crucifer or mustard family (Cruciferae), whose members have flowers with four petals arranged like a cross.

Cruciferae
The mustard family, formerly Brassicaceae. The family includes both ornamental plants and important vegetables, among them broccoli, cabbage, kale, and others in the genus *Brassica*.

Cryptomeria
The botanical name for Japanese cedar.

culm
A stem, especially of grasses, that is usually hollow except at the nodes. Bamboo is a good example.

culm

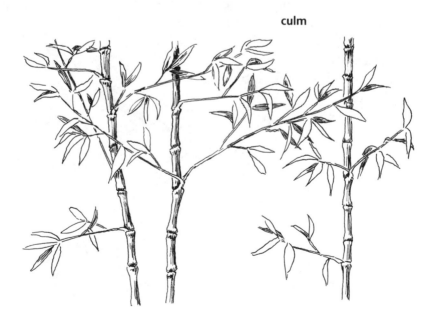

cultivar

A plant variety maintained in cultivation by vegetative propagation or from inbred seed. The word "cultivar" derives from "*culti*vated *var*iety." Cultivars have particular, desirable qualities that distinguish them from common, unselected seedlings. A cultivar name is indicated typographically by a roman word or words enclosed in single quotation marks. For example, there is only one species of heather, *Calluna vulgaris,* but there are hundreds of cultivars with flowers and foliage of different colors. If you want a heather with green foliage, pink flowers, and a mounding shape, you might select the cultivar *C. vulgaris* 'County Wicklow'. *See also* **hybrid; strain; species; variety.**

cultivate

To scratch or dig up the surface of the soil around plants in order to break the crust so water can penetrate, to eliminate weeds, or to conserve moisture by creating a dust mulch.

cultivator

A pronged tool for cultivating the soil.

cultivator

× *Cupressocyparis*

The botanical name for Leland cypress.

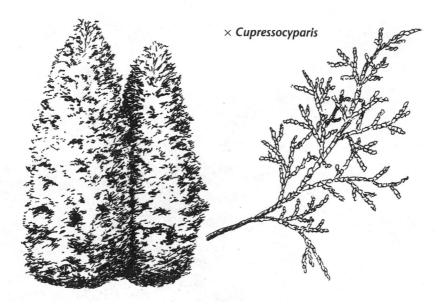

× *Cupressocyparis*

Cupressus
The botanical name for cypress.

cushion plant
See tufted.

cuticle
The waxy surface that reduces water loss from a leaf, evident on, for example, the leaves of rhododendrons and laurels.

cutting
A part of a plant removed from its parent and treated so that it produces roots and shoots and becomes a new plant. Most cuttings are taken from stems or shoots, but sometimes leaf or root cuttings are used.

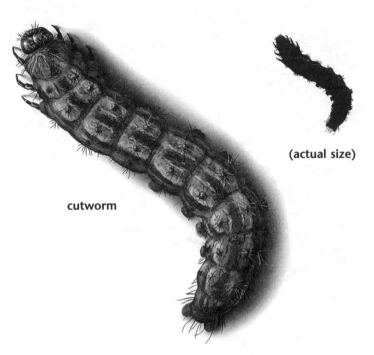

(actual size)

cutworm

cutting garden
A bed planted with annuals and other flowers that bloom
continuously or repeatedly, providing a supply of cut
flowers for the home.

cutworm
A smooth, wormlike, brown or green moth larva that feeds
near the soil, cutting off the stems of new transplants. A
cardboard collar placed around a seedling will keep
cutworms away from it.

Cymbidium
The orchid genus that includes the oldest cultivated
orchids.

cyme
A branched flower cluster that blooms from the center toward the edges.

Cypripedium
The botanical name for the lady's slipper orchid.

Cytisus
The botanical name for broom.

cytology
The scientific study of cells.

Cymbidium

damping-off
A common fungal disease that attacks seedlings, weakening the stems right at the soil level. Infected seedlings usually die. There is no cure, but prevention includes starting seeds in a sterile soil mix, using clean containers and tools, and providing good air circulation.

dappled shade
The sun-shade pattern cast by trees that are open enough to allow sun to penetrate between their leaves.

Dawes Arboretum
A 950-acre arboretum in Newark, Ohio, featuring more than 2,000 kinds of woody plants, including major collections of crab apples, pines, maples, oaks, hollies, and rhododendrons.

daylength
The number of hours from sunrise to sunset. Also called photoperiod.

daylength-sensitive
A term used to describe a plant whose flowering, dormancy, or other growth patterns are affected by daylight. *See also* **photoperiodism**.

day-neutral
A term used to describe a plant whose blooming period is not affected by the length of the day. *See also* **photoperiodism.**

deadheading
Removing old flowers during the growing season to encourage the development of new flowers and to prevent seed formation. Deadheading also improves the appearance of the garden. On the down side, removing seed heads may also mean depriving seed-eating birds of a favorite food — and depriving the gardener of the company of the birds.

deciduous
A term used to describe trees or shrubs that drop all their leaves to survive a cold or dry season; not evergreen.

declinate
Bent downward or forward.

decumbent
Lying on the ground but with growing tips turned upward.

deflexed
Bent or turned abruptly downward at a sharp angle, as is the habit of some weeping trees or shrubs.

decumbent

defoliant
A chemical that causes leaves to be shed. One use for defoliants is in the cotton fields, where fewer leaves make it easier to harvest the cotton bolls.

dehiscence
The splitting or other mode of opening of a seedpod for the release of seeds; the opening of an anther to discharge pollen. Fruits or anthers that never split are called indehiscent.

deltoides
As a species name, means "triangular." For example, eastern cottonwood, *Populus deltoides,* has triangular-shaped leaves.

Dendrobium
A hugely diverse orchid genus with more than 1,000 species, including some of the most beautiful of all orchids.

dendroid
Treelike in form but not in size.

dendrology
The botanical study of trees and other woody plants.

dense
Thick; compact; crowded together.

dentate
Toothed.

denticulate
Finely toothed.

Denver Botanic Gardens
A botanic garden comprising 40 distinct gardens, located just a few miles from the city's downtown skyscrapers. Notable are the Rock Alpine Garden, with more than 3,000 different plants, and the Xeriscape and Plains Gardens, which feature plants native only to Colorado.

Desert Botanical Garden
A garden located in Phoenix, Arizona, dedicated to the study of desert plants. It grows more than 1,000 kinds of cacti.

determinate
A term used to describe a plant whose terminal growth is stopped by the production of a flower and fruit cluster. Determinate tomato cultivars, for example, are compact plants that bear their entire crop over a short season. *See also* **indeterminate**.

Dianthus
The botanical name for pinks and carnations.

Dianthus

diatomaceous earth
An abrasive powder made from the shells of diatoms, sometimes used as an insecticide. The sharp particles damage soft-bodied larvae, snails, and slugs, causing them to lose moisture and die.

dibble
A pointed tool used to make holes in the soil, especially for planting bulbs and seedlings.

Dicentra
The botanical name for bleeding heart.

dichotomous
Forking into two equal branches at the growing point.

dicot
The common shortened form of the term "dicotyledon."

Digitalis

dicotyledon
A plant having two cotyledons in its seeds and usually
exhibiting a netlike pattern of veins in the leaf blades and
flower parts in groups of four or five. This group includes
all the broad-leaved trees and shrubs and many common
flowers such as daisies, phlox, carnations, and peonies.
See also **monocotyledon.**

Dictamnus
The botanical name for gas plant.

dieback
The death of a plant's stems, beginning at the tips, caused
by lack of water, nutrient deficiency, disease, frost damage,
insect attack, or injury from pruning.

dieback shrub
A tender shrub that can be grown in cold climates. It
freezes to the ground in winter but sends up new shoots
in spring.

diffuse
Of a loose, open habit.

Digitalis
The botanical name for foxglove.

dimorphic
A term used to describe a species that exists in two distinct
forms, sometimes seen on the same plant, such as English
ivy, whose juvenile and adult foliage are distinctly different.

dioecious
Having male and female flowers on separate plants.
Most hollies, junipers, and yews are dioecious. *See also*
monoecious.

dioicus, -a, -um
As a species name, means "having male and female flowers on separate plants." For example, in goatsbeard, *Aruncus dioicus,* the female plants have fluffy, drooping flower clusters and the males have thinner, feathery, upright plumes.

direct seeding
Sowing seeds directly in the soil where they are to grow, rather than transplanting seedlings.

dirt gardener
Anyone involved in the actual process of growing plants or working with the soil. The term had more relevance in the days when gardening might mean supervising a staff rather than doing the actual work oneself.

disbudding
Removing most of the immature buds from a plant to boost the size of the few selected to remain.

discolor
As a species name, means "of two different colors." For example, the pussy willow, *Salix discolor,* has leaves that are green on top and silvery on the bottom.

dish garden
A container planted with several species of indoor plants, designed to look like a garden scene.

disk
The center or cushion of a composite blossom, comprising many tiny florets packed close together. These make up the "eye" of a black-eyed Susan or daisy, for example. *See also* ray.

dissected
A term used to describe a leaf whose blade is divided into many slender segments, the clefts not reaching the midrib, as in some kinds of Japanese maples. *See also* **lobed; toothed.**

distressing the roots
The practice of cutting some of the outside roots on a root-bound container plant before setting it in the hole where it is to grow. If left untouched, the roots will continue to circle the ball and never grow out into the surrounding soil.

diurnal
A term used to describe a flower that opens only during the daytime.

divaricatus, -a, -um
As a species name, means "straggly, sprawling, or spreading." For example, wild sweet William, *Phlox divaricata,* has limp stems that flop over, and it also spreads to form a patch.

Phlox divaricata

division
The propagation of a plant by separating it into two or more pieces, each of which has at least one bud and some roots.

Dodecatheon
The botanical name for shooting star.

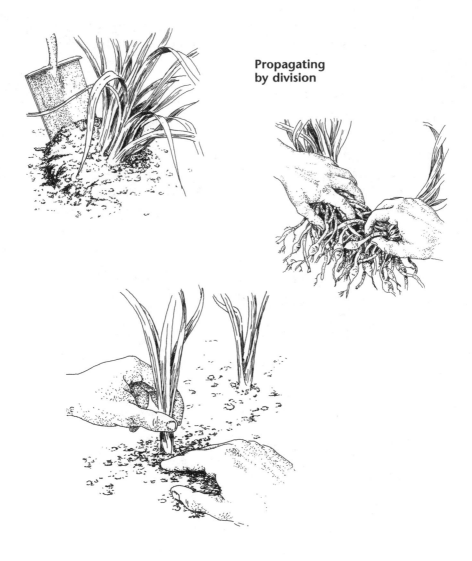

Propagating by division

dormancy
A state of reduced activity that enables plants to survive conditions of cold, drought, or other stress. Most plants drop their leaves before going dormant.

dormant oil
A light, thin, petroleum-based oil applied to fruit trees and other plants in winter to kill insects and insect eggs that are hidden on the bark and stems.

Doronicum
The botanical name for leopard's bane.

dorsal sepal
In orchids, the uppermost "petal" of a flower.

double digging
A method of deep cultivation by (1) digging out the top spade length (or "spit") of soil, (2) forking over and amending the lower level of soil, and (3) returning the topsoil to the hole on top of the cultivated lower level.

double-flowered
Having more than the usual number of petals, which are generally arranged in extra rows.

Douglas, David (1798–1834)
A Scot, one of the first botanists to explore the Pacific Northwest. Several plants were named in his honor, including the Douglas fir.

Downing, Andrew Jackson (1815–1852)
The first great American landscape architect. He adapted the romantic English style to the great estates along the Hudson River and on Long Island, New York. His picturesque landscapes were notable for their wild look—

woods, meadows, and rushing streams — and the rambling parks he designed for his wealthy clients were idealized versions of nature, complete with rolling meadows and artificial ponds surrounded by naturalized bulbs and wildflowers.

downy mildew
A disease caused by certain fungi (and not to be confused with powdery mildew or sooty mildew) and spread by windblown spores. It produces spots or fuzzy patches on the leaves of susceptible plants. Downy mildew is most troublesome in hot humid weather.

drainage
The movement of water down through the soil. Good drainage means water disappears from a planting hole in less than an hour. If water remains standing overnight or longer, the drainage is poor.

dried blood
A fairly fast-acting natural fertilizer containing about 10 percent nitrogen.

dried flower
See everlasting.

drift
A group of plants arranged in a graceful curved shape, spaced closer together in the center or at one end, then gradually farther apart at the edges or other end. Gertrude Jekyll was the first landscape designer to promote the idea of planting in drifts.

drill
A narrow trench in which seeds are planted or fertilizer is added near a row of seeds.

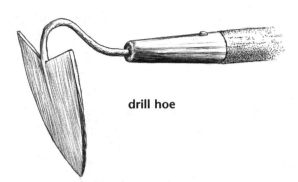

drill hoe

drill hoe
A hoe with a triangular blade, used to make the furrow in which seeds are planted.

drip feed
A system of pipes, hoses, and emitters that delivers a slow steady trickle of water and fertilizer onto the soil.

drip irrigation
A system similar to drip feed, except that it carries only water. Also called trickle irrigation.

drip line
An imaginary line on the soil around a tree that mirrors the circumference of the branches above. The feeder roots of a tree usually extend to or beyond this line and receive water that drips off the canopy above.

drooping
Pendent or hanging, as in the branches or shoots of a weeping willow.

Drosera
The botanical name for sundew.

drupe

A fleshy one-seeded fruit that does not split. The seed is enclosed in a bony stone; hence such fruits are often called stone fruits. Examples are peach, plum, cherry, and olive.

drupelets

Small drupes, such as those on a raspberry or blackberry, which are held together by nearly invisible hairs.

Dryopteris

The botanical name for a large genus of hardy or tropical ferns.

dry wall

A stone wall constructed without mortar. This construction was popular in colonial New England, where boundary walls were built by farmers from the large rocks that they had to dig out in order to plow the land (and which eventually drove them west, where the deep soil of the prairies proved more suitable for growing food crops than that of stony New England). Today the walls are an admired feature of the landscape, and in a garden, the cracks between the stones are ideal for growing small plants.

dry well

A hole filled with rocks and gravel, usually located beneath a drainpipe to absorb water that would otherwise flood the area.

Dumbarton Oaks

One of the great American gardens, located in Washington, D.C. The 1801 mansion was acquired by Mr. and Mrs. Robert Woods Bliss in 1920, and for a quarter of a century thereafter landscape architect Beatrix Farrand worked with the owners to perfect a series of formal gardens. The property was given to Harvard University in 1940 as a means of preserving the estate and the collections. It is open to the public.

dust mulch
Thoroughly pulverized surface soil, created by cultivating around plants, which is dried almost at once by sun and wind. Capillary water beneath this mulch cannot penetrate the dust layer and escape into the air. Thus a dust mulch conserves water at the plant roots, just as any other mulch does.

Dutch hoe
A hoe with a flat blade that works by being pushed away from the user.

dwarf
A plant that, due to inherited characteristics, is shorter and/or slower growing than the normal forms.

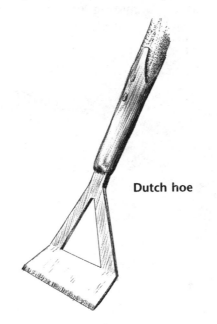

Dutch hoe

earthworm
The common name for several beneficial burrowing worms
that improve the soil as they burrow through the ground,
loosening and aerating it and helping to break down
organic matter.

earwig
A night-feeding insect that feeds primarily on decaying
matter and other insects, including aphids. Unfortunately,
earwigs also eat flowers.

earwig

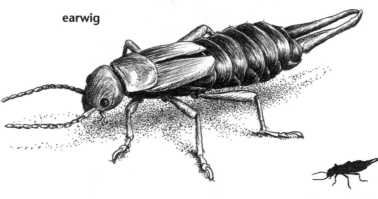

(actual size)

Echinacea

Echinacea
The botanical name for purple coneflower.

echinate
Bearing stiff prickly hairs.

ecology
1. The scientific study of the relationships between plants, animals, and their environment.
2. The study of the detrimental effects of modern civilization on the environment, with a view toward prevention or reversal through conservation.

ecosystem
A community of plants, animals, and their environment, functioning as a unit.

edging
A shallow trench or physical barrier of steel, plastic, brick, or boards used to define the border between a planting and adjacent turf.

edging plant
A neat, low-growing plant that spreads slowly, if at all, and looks good throughout the growing season. Can be annual, perennial, or shrubby. Used to create a ribbon- or hedgelike effect along the edge of a bed, next to a lawn or walkway.

edible landscaping
Growing vegetables, fruits, and herbs, often in combination with annual flowers, in beautiful, untraditional ways as part of the home landscape.

eel grass
Any of several aquatic grasses of the genus *Vallisneria*. As they age, they drift loose, wash up on the shore in piles, and turn black. They make an excellent mulch.

eelworm
See **nematode**.

embryo
The minute rudimentary plant contained within a seed.

encarsia wasp
A beneficial insect of the genus *Encarsia* that preys on the larvae of the whitefly.

endemic
Having a natural distribution confined to a particular geographic area.

entire
A term used to describe leaves that have a smooth edge with no teeth or lobes.

encarsia wasp

(actual size)

ephemeral
A plant that flowers for a very short time, such as a woodland plant that blooms in early spring before the trees leaf out and block the sunlight; a desert plant that blooms right after a rain.

epiphyte
A plant that is not a parasite but that attaches itself to another plant for support and uses its own aerial roots to collect food and water from the air. Many bromeliads are epiphytes, as are some orchids. Epiphytes are common in the tropics but rare in temperate climates.

epithet
See specific epithet.

Equisetum
The botanical name for horsetail and scouring rush.

Erica

erectus, -a, -um
As a species name, means "upright." For example, the African marigold, *Tagetes erecta*, a common annual bedding plant, has upright stems.

Eremurus
The botanical name for foxtail lily.

Erica
The botanical name for heath.

Ericaceae
The heath family, which includes many valuable broad-leaved evergreens, such as rhododendrons (and azaleas) and mountain laurels, as well as cranberries and blueberries. Most members of the heath family require acid soil.

ericaceous
Belonging to the heath family (Ericaceae), most of whose members prefer acid soil. Examples are azaleas, rhododendrons, blueberries, and heathers.

Erigeron
The botanical name for fleabane.

erythro-
As part of a species name, means "red." For example, new fronds of the Japanese autumn fern, *Dryopteris erythrosora,* have a reddish tint.

Erythronium
The botanical name for trout lily or dogtooth violet.

escape
A garden plant that has spread from cultivation and grows successfully in the wild.

Eschscholzia
The botanical name for California poppy and Mexican poppy.

Eschscholzia

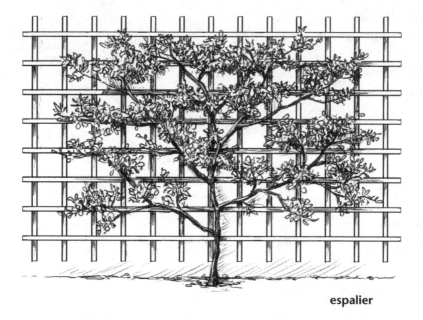

espalier

espalier
A shrub or tree that has been trained to grow flat against a wall or framework.

ethnobotany
The scientific study of the plant lore and agricultural customs of traditional societies.

ethylene
A gaseous plant hormone that promotes stem thickening and the development of flowers in some species.

etiolated
A term used to describe the condition of a plant that has been growing in darkness or even too little light. The stems are pale and elongated, and the leaves are small and widely spaced.

Eucalyptus
The botanical name for gum tree.

Eupatorium
The botanical name for Joe-Pye weed.

everblooming
A term often used to describe a rose that blooms nearly constantly from spring or early summer to fall.

Everett, Thomas H. (1903–1986)
One of the preeminent 20th-century horticulturists and educators, director of the New York Botanical Garden. On his retirement from that post in 1968, he spent 14 years writing the 3-million-word, 10-volume *New York Botanical Garden Illustrated Encyclopedia of Horticulture.* (He also took most of the 11,500 photographs.)

evergreen
A plant that retains its leaves for more than one annual cycle of growth.

Eupatorium

everlasting
A plant whose flowers can be prepared for dried arrangements.

exfoliating
A term used to describe bark that peels off in thin layers and has a patchy or shredded appearance.

exotic
A plant that is native to another part of the world but has been introduced here. Some exotics, such as Japanese honeysuckle and purple loosestrife, have escaped from gardens to become serious pests in parts of the country.

exposure
The intensity, duration, and variation in sun, wind, and temperature that characterize any particular site.

eye
1. A bud on a cutting, tuber, or tuberous root; for example, the eyes on a potato.
2. A dark spot in the center of a flower, as seen in black-eyed Susans and many kinds of pinks and primroses.

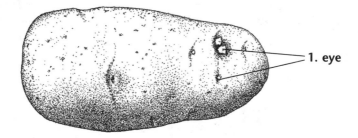

1. eye

F₁ hybrid
A first-generation offspring of two plants of closely related species or strains. (The "F" stands for "filial.") The resulting plants are usually more vigorous than either parent and have other qualities that are considered more desirable. However, the seeds produced by an F₁ hybrid will rarely produce plants of comparable value.

F₂ hybrid
A cross between two F₁ hybrids. This second-generation cross does not produce consistent or vigorous plants.

Fagus
The botanical name for beech.

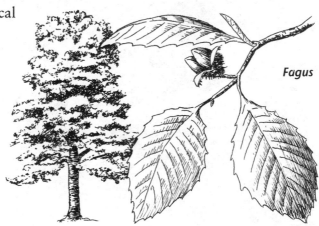

Fagus

Fairchild Tropical Garden
The largest tropical botanical garden in the United States, located in Coral Gables, Florida. Although it was in the direct destructive path of Hurricane Andrew in 1992, the 83-acre garden has survived and still has one of the world's greatest collections of palms and cycads.

fairy ring
A circle in a grassy area marking the periphery of an underground fungal growth. The name comes from an old belief that such manifestations were a dancing ground for fairies. Fairy rings can range in size from a few inches to as much as a hundred yards in diameter.

falcate
Sickle shaped.

fall
The drooping lower petal of the flowers of irises and related plants.

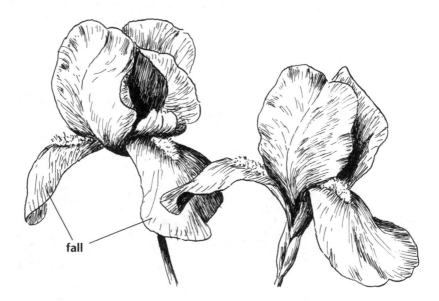

fall

family

A group of plants above the category of genus, defined by characteristics of flowers and fruits. Important examples are the grass, lily, mint, and daisy families (respectively, Gramineae, Liliaceae, Labiatae, and Compositae).

Farrand, Beatrix Jones (1872–1959)

American landscape designer whose most famous commissions included the Dumbarton Oaks estate in Washington, D.C. (now open to the public); gardens at the White House; and the campuses of Yale and Princeton universities. At her summer home in Bar Harbor, Maine, she designed extensive gardens, established a horticultural library, and assembled an outstanding collection of plants.

fasciation

An abnormal widening and flattening of a stem, typically of a flower stalk. While generally of unknown origin, it is sometimes due to disease. Fasciation is often found in the genera *Nicotiana, Celosia,* and *Lilium.*

fastigiate

With the branches turning upward and relatively close to the trunk. Fastigiate trees are rare or unknown in the wild but popular in gardens. The Lombardy poplar, *Populus nigra* 'Italica', is a good example.

fastigiate

feeder roots
A dense network of slender branching roots that spread close to the surface of the soil and absorb most of the nutrients for a tree or shrub.

felted
Covered with short dense hairs.

female
A plant having only pistillate flowers.

fern
A nonflowering plant that reproduces by spores, not seeds, and that has fronds, not leaves.

Fernwood Botanical Gardens
A 105-acre botanic garden and arboretum in Niles, Michigan, featuring more than 3,000 species of native and exotic plants that grow well in the Great Lakes region.

fertile
1. A term used to describe soil that has a ready supply of nitrogen, phosphorus, potassium, and the other nutrients needed by plants. To fertilize plants is to supply these nutrients.
2. A term used to describe a seed that has an embryo capable of developing into a new plant. To fertilize flowers is to transfer pollen from the anther of one flower to the stigma of the same or a different flower.

fertilizer
A substance that contains one or more of the necessary plant nutrients.

Festuca
The botanical name for fescue.

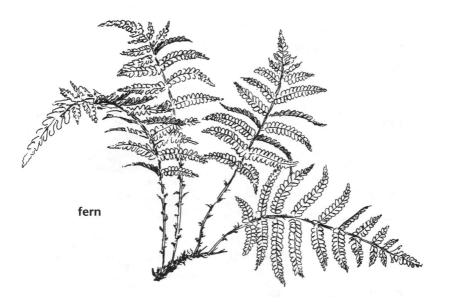

fern

Fiacre, Saint

In an unlikely combination, the patron saint of gardeners
and Paris taxi drivers. He is often represented carrying a
shovel. A hermit at Kilfiachra in Ireland, he was given land
near Paris by the bishop of Meaux. He built a monastery
there and grew vegetables and flowers; his fame as a
gardener and a spiritual healer brought him visitors and
pilgrims from all over France, until his death in 670. In the
17th century, there was a revival of his fame, and pilgrims
came to the chapel where he was buried, traveling by hired
coaches known as fiacres. The first taxi stand in Paris was
said to be near the Hotel St. Fiacre, and today Paris taxis
are still known as fiacres.

fiber

One of the elongated, thick-walled cells that give strength
and support to plant tissue.

fibril

A root hair; a small fiber.

fibrous roots
Fine root hairs that are highly branched and often matted, as opposed to thick fleshy roots.

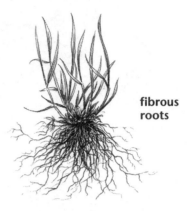

fibrous
roots

fibrous tissue
Tissue made up of fibers.

Ficus
The botanical name for fig.

filament
The slender stalk that supports the pollen-bearing anther.

filamentosus, -a, -um
As a species name, means "having filaments or threads." For example, the leaves of bear grass, *Yucca filamentosa*, contain stiff, strong white fibers that Native Americans spun into thread and twine.

filiform
Long and thin; threadlike.

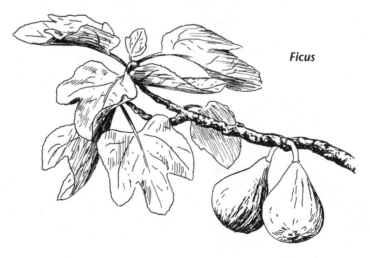

Ficus

Filipendula

Filipendula
The botanical name for meadowsweet.

Filoli Center
A public garden located in Woodside, California, that is a reflection of the opulent style of the houses and gardens of wealthy San Franciscans in the early days of the 20th century. It is also one of the rare California gardens that remain true to their original plan. "Filoli" is an acronym from the words "fidelity," "love," and "life."

fimbriate
Fringed, as the edge of a frilly petal or a leaf.

fire ant
An aggressive ant that forms large colonies in fields, gardens, and lawns across the South. Fire ants do not harm plants, but they bite gardeners, and once they have entered an area, it is hard to get rid of them.

fire blight
A bacterial disease of apple, pear, firethorn, hawthorn, and related plants. The disease causes sudden browning and death of small branches or entire limbs of trees.

firm
To press down the soil after planting, in order to eliminate air pockets and to secure the plant in place.

first true leaves
The first leaves produced by a seedling that have the arrangement and appearance typical of that species. *See also* **seed leaf.**

fish emulsion
A liquid organic fertilizer made from fish wastes.

fistulose
Hollow and tubular, as the leaf of a scallion or a bamboo culm.

flask-grown
A term used to describe a plant (especially an orchid) grown via micropropagation techniques such as mericloning, or meristem propagation, and thus a clone of some original plant; not seed-grown.

flat
A shallow tray for starting seeds or for holding or carrying cell packs or pots.

flea beetle
A tiny dark beetle that feeds on foliage and can do considerable damage to seedlings, particularly in vegetable gardens. When disturbed, these insects hop like fleas.

flea beetle

(actual size)

flesh
The pulpy, usually edible part of a fruit or vegetable.

flocculate
To cause soil to form clumps or masses. Adding gypsum to clay soil makes it fluffier, better drained, and easier to work with.

flora
All the kinds of plants, both native and exotic, that grow wild in an area.

flore pleno
As a species, cultivar, or variety name, means "having double flowers." For example, *Sanguinaria canadensis* 'Flore Pleno' is a rare form of bloodroot with large, double flowers.

floret
A small flower, especially one in a cluster or an inflorescence, as in the grass and daisy families (respectively, Gramineae and Compositae).

floribundus, -a, -um or *floridus, -a, -um*

As a species name, describes plants that flower abundantly, making showy displays, such as Japanese andromeda, *Pieris floribunda,* or flowering dogwood, *Cornus florida.*

floriculture

Strictly speaking, the raising of flowers, as distinguished from general horticulture. Generally, the term has come to mean any branch of horticulture that has to do with ornamental plants.

floriferous

Literally, having flowers. In common usage the term is used to describe a plant with an abundance of flowers.

florilegium

Originally, a collection of flowers. Today the term typically denotes a book about plants.

floristic provinces

Regions that have similar growing conditions. For example, in the United States and Canada, the regions are usually described as Eastern Woodlands; Coastal Plain; Great Plains; Western Deserts; California Province; and Western Mountains and Pacific Northwest.

-florus, -a, -um

As part of a species name, refers to the flowers. For example, glossy abelia, *Abelia × grandiflora,* has larger flowers than other abelias do.

flower

The reproductive organ of most garden plants. Flowers are often large and bright-colored to attract pollinators but are sometimes quite small and inconspicuous. Regardless of appearance, a flower is successful if it produces viable seeds.

flower head

An inflorescence that appears to be a single flower but that is actually made up of a dense cluster of florets. Members of the composite family (Compositae), such as daisy and tansy, have flower heads.

flush

A sudden burst of bloom, usually of flowers or fruit.

Foeniculum

The botanical name for fennel.

foetidus, -a, -um

As a species name, means "bad-smelling." For example, stinking hellebore, *Helleborus foetidus,* has flowers that smell mildly unpleasant if you get close to them.

foliage plant

A plant that is grown primarily for its handsome leaves. Coleus and caladium are examples.

**foliage plant
(caladium)**

foliar feeding

Spraying a liquid fertilizer solution on leaves, rather than applying it to the soil for uptake via the roots, as is the usual practice.

-folius, -a, -um

As part of a species name, refers to the leaves. For example, fountain butterfly bush, *Buddleia alternifolia,* has alternate leaves.

follicle

A dry, single-chambered fruit that splits along only one seam to release its seeds, as in larkspur and milkweed.

folly

A nonfunctional but decorative and usually romantic garden structure, such as an artificial ruin, a popular feature of grand 18th-century estate gardens.

foot-candle

The illumination produced by a candle at a distance of 1 foot. This unit of measure is useful in determining the amount of artificial light needed by houseplants or seedlings grown indoors.

forb

A broad-leaved herbaceous plant that grows alongside grasses in a field, prairie, or meadow.

forcing

Artificially adjusting the light and temperature to accelerate the flowering of a plant.

fork

1. A digging or lifting tool with tines instead of a solid head like a spade.

2. The point at which two branches of approximately equal size divide. *See also* **crotch**.

form
A subdivision of a variety, differing in only one characteristic, such as the color of the flower.

formal garden
A garden laid out in regular geometric patterns with defined paths and pruned hedges.

Fortune, Robert (1812–1880)
A Scottish horticulturist who traveled and lived in China for many years and introduced dozens of Chinese plants to Western gardens, including the lovely *Rhododendron fortunei,* which has large, fragrant, pink flowers. He also worked for the East India Company and, despite the opposition of the Chinese government, managed to get tea plants out of China and establish the first tea plantations in India and Ceylon (now Sri Lanka).

foundation planting
A narrow border of generally evergreen shrubs planted around the foundation of a house.

Fragaria
The botanical name for strawberry.

Fragaria

fragrans
As a species name, means "fragrant or sweet-scented." For example, sweet olive, *Osmanthus fragrans,* has tiny flowers with a delightful aroma.

Fraxinus
The botanical name for ash.

French intensive gardening
An approach to vegetable gardening that produces maximum harvests from a small plot. It was introduced to the United States by Alan Chadwick, who established a teaching and demonstration center in Santa Cruz, California, and was further popularized by one of Chadwick's students, John Jeavons, who wrote the book *How to Grow More Vegetables Than You Ever Thought Possible on Less Land Than You Can Imagine.*

Fraxinus

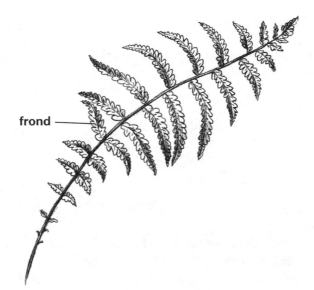

frond

friable
A term used to describe soil texture that is loose and
crumbly, easily penetrated by roots and water. *See also*
tilth.

frond
The leaflike part of a fern; the leaf of a palm.

frost-free days
The number of days from the last spring frost to the first
fall frost. This measure of the length of a growing season
for plants that cannot survive the cold is most significant to
gardeners who wish to grow tender annual flowers and
vegetables.

frost heaving
See **heaving.**

frost pocket
A low-lying place where late and early frosts are more
likely than in the surrounding areas. *See also* **microclimate.**

fruit
The mature or ripened ovary of a flower, containing one or more seeds.

fruit fly
Any of various tiny flies that lay eggs on fruit. The larvae bore into the ripe fruit and cause it to rot.

fruiting body
An organ in fungi and mosses that produces spores.

frutescens, fruticans, or ***fruticosus, -a, -um***
As a species name, means "shrubby or bushy." For example, Jerusalem sage, *Phlomis fruticosa,* is a shrubby perennial with stems that get woody at the base.

fruticose
Shrubby; resembling a shrub.

fulgens or ***fulgidus, -a, -um***
As a species name, means "shining or glistening." For example, the perennial black-eyed Susan or coneflower,

fruit fly larvae

Rudbeckia fulgida, has shiny gold ray florets (often mistakenly called petals).

full shade
The shade beneath the branches of mature, spreading trees.

full sun
A term used to describe a location that receives a minimum of six hours of direct sun each day during the growing season.

fungicide
A compound that inhibits the growth of fungal organisms. Fungicides rarely kill fungi and are more useful as a preventive than as a cure.

fungus (plural: fungi)
Any of a number of plants that lack chlorophyll and that feed on organic matter. Common fungi include yeasts, molds, and mushrooms. Some are beneficial, but others are the cause of plant diseases and many are poisonous to humans.

furcate
Forked.

furrow
A narrow ditch made by a spade or a plough, usually to receive seeds or to direct water runoff.

fusarium
A soilborne fungal disease that affects a wide variety of herbaceous plants, causing wilting and death. *See also* V,F,N.

Gaillardia
The botanical name for blanket flower.

Galanthus
The botanical name for snowdrop.

Galium
The botanical name for sweet woodruff.

Galium

gall

gall
An abnormal growth on a plant, usually caused by insects but sometimes by fungi or bacteria. *See also* **crown gall**.

gamete
A sex cell, either sperm or egg, capable of fusing with another gamete of the opposite sex to form a fertilized egg.

Garden Conservancy, The
An organization formed in 1989 for the primary purpose of preserving exceptional American gardens by facilitating their transfer from private to independent, nonprofit, public ownership and management.

garden designer
Someone who makes a business of designing gardens, draws up plans, designs simple hardscape projects, and decides what plants to grow where. Unlike landscape architects, garden designers are often self-taught and are not licensed by states. Also called landscape designer.

Garden-in-the-Woods
See **New England Wild Flower Society**.

Gaultheria
The botanical name for wintergreen.

gazebo
A roofed, open-sided structure, usually round or octagonal, used as a shady resting place in a garden.

generic
Of or relating to a genus.

genus (plural: genera)
A group of plant species with similarities in flower form and often in general appearance, growth habit, and cultural requirements. A genus may include from one to a thousand or more species. The name of the genus is the first word in the two-part Latin plant name. The common names for many groups of plants, such as aster, cosmos, magnolia, and rhododendron, are also the Latin names for those genera. *See also* **Linnaeus, Carolus; species.**

geotropism
The movement of plant parts in response to gravity. Positive geotropism causes roots to grow downward; negative geotropism causes stems to grow upward.

Gerard, John (1545–1612)
English botanist and barber-surgeon. His 1596 catalog of the plants in his garden was the first of its kind to be published. He is best known for his 1597 *Herball,* largely an adaptation of other works to which he added folklore and observations.

germination
The initial sprouting of a seed.

gibberellin
A plant hormone that can be artificially applied to affect the formation of flowers and the size of fruit.

gill
One of the finlike structures on the underside of the cap of a mushroom.

girdle
To remove or damage the bark (both outer bark and inner bark) in a ring extending completely around a trunk or shoot of a tree or shrub. This kills the plant—not immediately, but in the subsequent growing season.

girdling root
A root of a woody plant grown in a round nursery pot that starts to grow in a coil or spiral pattern, wrapping around the inside of the pot. Such roots should be cut off altogether or pulled loose and straightened out when the tree or shrub is planted. If not removed or redirected, a girdling root can eventually strangle a plant by constricting the growth of the other roots and, more important, of the trunk or main shoots.

girdling root

Giverny
The home and garden of the French artist Claude Monet.
The garden was an inspiration for some of Monet's most
memorable paintings.

glaber, -ra, -um
As a species name, means "smooth or hairless." For
example, turtlehead, *Chelone glabra,* has smooth leaves.

glabrous
Smooth, having no hairs or fuzz.

glade
An open space in a woodland.

glasshouse
The British term for greenhouse.

glaucous
Covered with a grayish, bluish, or whitish waxy coating or
bloom that is easily brushed off.

glaucus, -a, -um
As a species name, means "having leaves or other parts
with a white coating." For example, the white spruce, *Picea
glauca,* is not white, but its needles are lighter colored than
those of other spruces because they are covered with a
waxy white film.

Gleditzia
The botanical name for honey locust.

glen
A narrow valley.

gracilis, -e

As a species name, means "graceful or slender." For example, *Deutzia gracilis,* a deciduous shrub, has slender twigs that form a graceful, arching mound.

grade

1. The degree and direction of slope on a piece of ground.
2. To smooth or level a piece of ground.

grafting

Joining a bud or shoot from one plant onto the roots or trunk of another plant so that the two parts will unite and grow together.

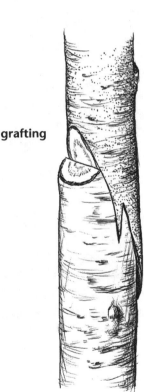

grafting

graft union

The place on the stem of a plant where the scion, or bud, is joined to the rootstock or trunk. It is usually indicated by a slight swelling. Also called union or bud union.

Gramineae

The grass family, one of the largest and most economically important families of flowering plants, including grains and bamboos. Also called Poaceae.

grandi-

As part of a species name, means "large." For example, Chinese trumpet creeper, *Campsis grandiflora,* has large flowers. The giant fir, *Abies grandis,* can grow over 200 feet tall.

**ground cover
(pachysandra)**

granular fertilizer
Dry, pelleted fertilizer that can be mixed into the soil or spread over the surface of a garden bed. Both natural and synthetic fertilizers are available in granular form.

graveolens
As a species name, means "heavy-scented." For example, dill, *Anethum graveolens,* has aromatic foliage, flowers, and seeds.

Gray, Asa (1810–1888)
The leading American botanist of the 19th century. As professor of natural history at Harvard from 1842, he taught many who became eminent botanists, and he popularized the subject through his articles and textbooks.

gray mold
See botrytis.

greenhouse
A structure, covered with glass, fiberglass, or plastic, in which temperature and humidity can be controlled, for the cultivation and/or protection of plants.

green manure
A quick-growing crop, such as buckwheat, clover, rye, or other grain or legume, that is cut down and turned into the soil, where it decomposes and provides nutrients and humus. The best plants for this purpose produce a large amount of top growth and an extensive root system within a few months after seeding. *See also* **cover crop.**

Grevillea
The botanical name for silk oak tree.

grex
Particularly in orchid nomenclature, a term used to refer to the progeny of a specific cross.

ground cover
A plant such as English ivy, lilyturf, or pachysandra used to cover the soil and form a continuous low mass of foliage. Ground covers are often used as durable, undemanding substitutes for turfgrass.

growing medium
See **medium.**

growing on
Caring for a seedling or rooted cutting that has recently been transplanted into a larger pot.

growing point
The tip of a stem where new growth occurs. When it is pinched off, side shoots usually develop below this point.

growing season
The average number of days from the last spring frost to the first fall frost. *See also* **frost-free days.**

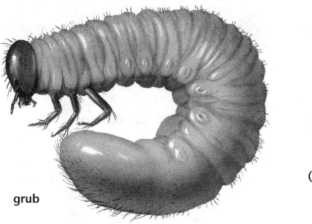

(actual size)

grub

growth regulator
A chemical used to alter the natural growth of plants. Growth regulators are used by nurseries to dwarf plants or to make the stems shorter.

growth retardant
A chemical sprayed on plants to reduce their size. Growth retardants are commonly used by growers to dwarf potted plants such as chrysanthemums and poinsettias.

growth ring
See **annual ring**.

grub
The larva of many kinds of beetles, including the Japanese beetle. Many grubs live underground and eat plant roots.

grub out
To clear an area of roots and stumps.

guano
Bird droppings, used as manure.

gymnosperms
One of the two largest groups of plants in the plant kingdom (the other is the angiosperms, or flowering plants). Gymnosperms, which typically form their seeds in the open spaces of cones, include all the conifers as well as the cycads. *See also* **angiosperms.**

Gypsophila
The botanical name for baby's breath.

gypsum
A mineral, calcium sulfate, that is used to add calcium to the soil or to improve the structure of clay soils without affecting the pH. *See also* **flocculate.**

gypsy moth
A type of silk moth accidentally introduced into the United States from Europe. The larvae of the gypsy moth feed on the leaves of hardwood trees and, in a bad infestation, can completely defoliate a forest.

gypsy moth

(actual size)

habit
The characteristic shape or form of a plant, such as upright, spreading, or rounded.

habitat
The area or type of environment in which a plant or an ecological community normally lives or occurs.

ha-ha
A deep ditch surrounding the grounds of an 18th- or 19th-century English manor house, intended to keep animals out. It was built to be invisible from the house so as not to interrupt the view. A modern version, sometimes used by gardeners to keep deer out, is the cattle crossing grate.

Halesia
The botanical name for silver-bell tree.

half-hardy
A term used to describe annuals such as sweet alyssum (or perennials that are treated as annuals, such as snapdragons) that can tolerate a slight frost without damage, either when set out in the spring as seedlings or as mature plants in the fall.

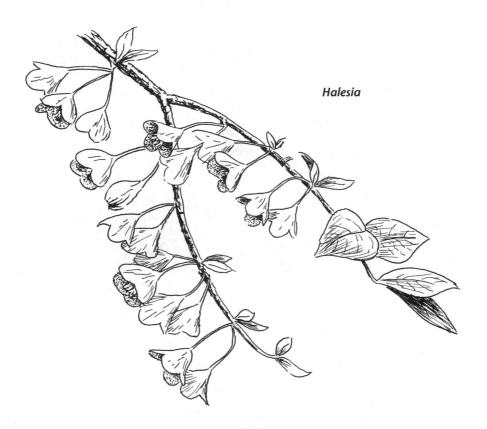

Halesia

half-ripened
A term used to describe the current year's wood on a plant still in active growth.

half shade
An area in which plants receive doses of full sun alternating with doses of full shade. Also called part shade; part sun.

halophyte
A plant that tolerates a large amount of salt in the soil. Plants that live on coastal dunes or in salt marshes are halophytes.

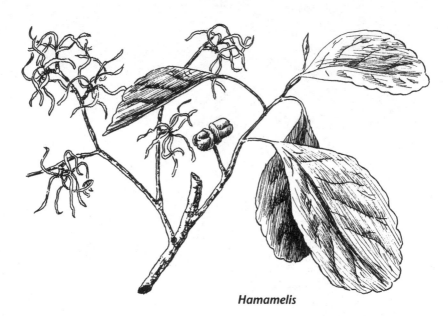

Hamamelis

Hamamelis
The botanical name for witch hazel.

hardening off
Gradually exposing a plant that has been growing under
sheltered conditions to cold, heat, sun, and wind. Seedlings
started indoors must be hardened off before they are
planted in the open ground.

hardiness
1. Also called cold-hardiness. A plant's ability to withstand
   cold winter weather. Hardiness is commonly specified as
   the minimum temperature to which a particular plant
   can be exposed and still be able to resume growth.
   Thus a plant may be said to be hardy to, for example,
   32 degrees, 10 degrees, or 0 degrees F. Often different
   parts of a plant are more or less hardy, and sometimes
   these are rated separately. For instance, growers of

rhododendrons, fruit trees, and other specialties may note one temperature that kills the flower buds, a colder temperature that kills the leaves and the tips of the stems, and an even colder temperature that kills the whole plant, roots and all. Most gardeners are content with simpler systems that assign plants to hardiness zones. *See also* **hardiness zones.**

2. A term sometimes used to refer to a plant's endurance of environmental conditions other than cold, such as summer heat or drought.

hardiness zones
A system for rating the cold-hardiness of plants, issued by the United States Department of Agriculture and recently revised and updated. This system divides the United States and Canada into eleven zones, based on average minimum temperatures in winter. For example, in USDA Zone 5, average winter lows are between −10 and −20 degrees Fahrenheit. Typically, a plant that is rated as hardy to USDA Zone 5 is also hardy in USDA Zone 6 and warmer zones but not in Zone 4 or colder zones. The USDA Hardiness Zone Map, which shows the boundaries of all the zones, is regularly printed in plant catalogs and garden books. *See also* **climate zones.**

hardpan
A layer of compacted subsoil that often prevents the penetration of water or of shrub or tree roots. Hardpan can occur naturally or be caused by repeated cultivation with a tiller or plow.

hardscape
The permanent features in a garden that are built from wood, stone, brick, or other durable materials, such as patios, walkways, fences, or trellises.

hardwood
The wood produced by broad-leaved flowering trees or shrubs such as maples and oaks, used as timber, lumber, or firewood. *See also* **softwood**.

hardwood cutting
A cutting of the previous season's growth taken from a dormant tree or shrub.

hardy
A term used to describe a plant that is able to survive freezing temperatures. Hardiness depends on geographic location, expressed in hardiness zones. Thus a perennial, shrub, or tree that is hardy in Zone 6 may not be hardy in Zone 5. Annual plants rated as hardy can be set out before the last frost. *See also* **hardiness zones**.

Hardy Plant Society
A society that originated in England but now has rapidly growing chapters in the United States, based in the Philadelphia area and the Portland, Oregon, area. Members are avid amateur or professional gardeners who collect and grow unusual and desirable herbaceous perennials in order to determine their hardiness and suitability for American gardens.

hay
Dried stems of grass and other herbaceous plants, sometimes used as an ingredient in compost or as a mulch. Hay supplies organic matter and some nutrients to the soil, but it is likely to contain seeds, including weed seeds, that will germinate and grow wherever it is spread. Hay sold as "mulch hay" or "spoiled hay" is cheaper than hay sold for animal feed, either because it has been rained on and

gotten moldy, which is still fine for garden use, or because it contains coarse, unpalatable stalks and seed heads, which are undesirable. Experienced gardeners regard hay with caution. *See also* **salt marsh hay; straw.**

heading back   **heading back**
A method of limiting the height of tall, floppy perennials and encouraging them to branch out. When they reach one-third of their usual mature size, they may be cut back by about one-third. Also, a method of severely pruning fruit trees by cutting back all the branches.

heading cut
In pruning, the removal of the tip of a stem or branch, to encourage bushiness or a spreading habit.

heart rot
Decay of internal plant tissues, which occurs most commonly in root vegetables or trees.

heartwood
The dead wood at the center of a trunk or branch of a tree. Although it no longer sustains the tree's life by conducting water, it does supply support.

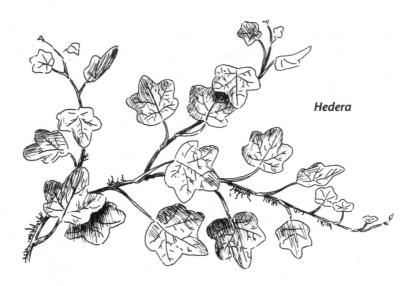

Hedera

heath
Open land with few trees and covered with scrub and other low plants. A term rarely used in North America.

heaving
The uprooting in winter of newly planted or shallow-rooted specimens caused by the alternate freezing and thawing of the soil. Also called frost heaving.

heavy soil
Clay soil that is dense, not friable.

Hedera
The botanical name for ivy.

hedge
A closely spaced row of one species of shrubs or trees that make a continuous border or barrier around a property or part of a garden. Hedges can be sheared or not.

hedgerow
As distinguished from a hedge, generally a mixture of assorted trees and/or shrubs.

Hedychium
The botanical name for ginger lily.

heel cutting
A cutting made from a side shoot with part of the main stem attached.

heeling in
Temporarily storing a plant by covering its roots with soil.

heeling in

heirloom plant
Not a precise term, but generally a cultivar of a flowering plant or vegetable that has been in cultivation for at least 50 years.

Helenium

Helenium
The botanical name for sneezeweed.

Helianthus
The botanical name for sunflower.

Helichrysum
The botanical name for everlasting.

heliotropism
See **phototropism**.

Hemerocallis
The botanical name for daylily.

herb
Technically, a herbaceous plant, one that does not form a woody stem. More popularly, herbs are "useful" plants, grown for their fragrance, medicinal properties, or culinary attributes. Under this definition, an herb may be herbaceous, like parsley, or woody, like rosemary.

Hemerocallis

herbaceous

1. Green and leaflike in appearance and texture.
2. Having aboveground stems that are fleshy, as opposed to woody.

herbaceous border

The English term for perennial border. Such plantings were invented by Gertrude Jekyll as an alternative to the popular Victorian style of carpet bedding with annuals.

**herb
(chamomile)**

herbaceous perennial

Often simply referred to as a perennial, a nonwoody plant
that may last anywhere from a few years (short-lived
perennial) to decades. Many herbaceous perennials are
evergreen, especially where winters are mild, but others go
dormant and die down to the ground for part of the year.
Although their tops are dead, their roots live on below the
ground; it is from these persistent rootstocks that the plants
renew themselves every year. *See also* **perennial; woody
perennial.**

herbal

An old, usually pre-Linnaean book containing lists and
descriptions of herbs. Although the herbalists who wrote
these volumes made many quaint mistakes about plants
and their "virtues," the great value of these mostly 16th-
century German and British books is that they contain a
complete description of what was cultivated at the time.

herbarium

An institution that houses a collection of dried plants
mounted, labeled, and systematically arranged for scientific
study.

herbicide

A chemical used to kill plants. Selective herbicides kill only
particular kinds of plants. Nonselective herbicides kill or
damage a wide range of plants.

Herb Society of America

A major organization devoted to the study and use of
herbs. It has 35 chapters and maintains the Herb Garden at
the National Arboretum in Washington, D.C.

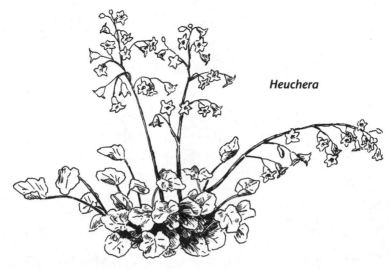

Heuchera

heterosis
See hybrid vigor.

Heuchera
The botanical name for coralbells or alumroot.

Hibiscus
The botanical name for mallow.

high-centered
As applied to roses, having the central petals longest. The classic hybrid tea rose form.

high shade
The shade beneath a tree that has been limbed up, by nature or the gardener, to 20 feet or more above ground level.

hill up
To pull up the soil around the growing stem of a plant.

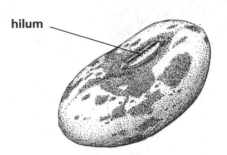

hilum

hilum
The scar on a seed coat marking the place where it was attached to the ovary during development.

hip
The closed and ripened firm or fleshy fruit of a rose, containing the seeds and often brightly colored.

hirtus, -a, -um or *hirsutus, -a, -um*
As a species name, means "covered with stiff bristly hairs" (not soft and fuzzy). For example, the annual black-eyed Susan or gloriosa daisy, *Rudbeckia hirta,* bears leaves and stems that have a rough texture because they are covered with short stiff hairs.

hoe
Any one of a number of long-handled tools used to loosen the soil or to cut out weeds.

Holden Arboretum
A huge arboretum in Mentor, Ohio, with more than 7,000 kinds of plants on almost 3,000 acres. It specializes in ornamental fruit trees, rhododendrons, and other trees and shrubs but has wildflower and perennial displays, too.

holdfast
An aerial rootlet on the stems of certain vines, such as English ivy, that enables the vine to climb by attaching itself to a masonry wall.

honeydew
The sweet sticky material secreted by aphids and other sap-sucking insects.

horizon
A layer of soil in the soil profile. *See* **soil profile**.

hort-
As part of a species name, means "associated with gardens." It usually identifies a group of plants that have been hybridized repeatedly and cultivated for so long that their ancestry is untraceable. For example, *Pelargonium* × *hortorum* is a catchall species that includes the common geraniums grown as bedding plants or houseplants.

horticultural oil
A light, highly refined mineral oil, mixed with water and used as an insecticidal spray. *See also* **dormant oil**.

horticulture
The cultivation of plants for ornament or food.

Hortus
A dictionary of plants cultivated in the United States and Canada, initially compiled by Liberty Hyde Bailey in 1930 and twice revised and expanded by the staff of the L. H. Bailey Hortorium of Cornell University.

hortus conclusus
An enclosed medieval garden.

hose-in-hose

hose-in-hose
A peculiar form of flower that appears to have a second flower growing from its center. Examples include some primroses, certain Kurume azaleas, and some forms of Canterbury bells.

host
The plant that supports a parasite. For example, oak trees often serve as hosts to mistletoe, a parasitic plant.

Hosta
The botanical name for plantain lily.

hotbed
A glass-enclosed bed of soil heated with fermenting manure or — more likely these days — an electric cable, used to germinate seeds or to protect seedlings or tender plants.

hot cap
An individual cone-shaped cover made of translucent
waxed paper or plastic, used to protect new plants against
cold weather or from birds.

hot compost
Compost prepared in such a way that it was heated to
temperatures as high as 160 degrees F for several days or
longer as it decomposed, hot enough to kill weed seeds and
disease organisms. *See also* **cold compost; compost.**

hothouse
A heated greenhouse.

houseplant
Any plant that is typically grown indoors. Most
houseplants are native to tropical regions. Also called pot
plant.

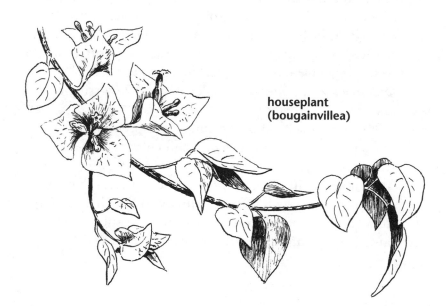

**houseplant
(bougainvillea)**

humilis, -e
As a species name, means "low-growing or dwarf." For example, the European fan palm, *Chamaerops humilis,* forms a bushy clump and never develops a tall trunk.

humus
Organic matter derived from partially decomposed plant and animal remains. It is an important constituent of garden soil.

Huntington Botanical Gardens
Extensive plantings on over 200 acres in San Marino, California, featuring a huge landscaped display of cacti and succulents, plus roses, camellias, and many other ornamentals.

hybrid
A plant resulting from a cross between two parents that belong to different varieties, cultivars, species, or (rarely) genera. A hybrid may show some of the characteristics of each parent or have a new appearance. Hybrid species are indicated by a roman multiplication sign (×) written before the species name. For example, the hybrid witch hazel, *Hamamelis × intermedia,* was developed by crossing two Asian species, *H. japonica* and *H. mollis.*

For hybrid cultivars, sometimes the species name is omitted and just the genus name and cultivar name are given, as for hybrid daylilies such as *Hemerocallis* 'Hyperion'. Omitting the species name indicates that the parentage is uncertain or too complex to list, or that only one offspring resulted from a cross and the subsequent plants have been propagated by vegetative means.

Hypericum

hybrid vigor
The tendency of many hybrids to grow faster, get larger, bear more flowers and fruit, or be more adaptable than their parents. Also called heterosis.

hydroponics
See **soilless gardening**.

hydroseeding
A method of sowing grass seed in a stream of water aimed at the ground to be covered. It is particularly useful for large-scale properties or land that is on a steep hillside.

Hypericum
The botanical name for St.-John's-wort.

hypertufa
A man-made imitation of lightweight tufa rock, which can be used in rock gardens or molded into planters. It is made by mixing dry cement, sand or perlite, peat moss, and water.

Iberis
The botanical name for candytuft.

iffy
According to nurseryman and writer Frederick McGourty, "a wonderful word conceived and propagated by rock gardeners." Generally, an iffy plant is one that may or may not survive in your own garden (while maddeningly flourishing for someone else).

ikebana
The Japanese art of formal flower arrangement, with special regard shown to balance, harmony, and form.

ikebana

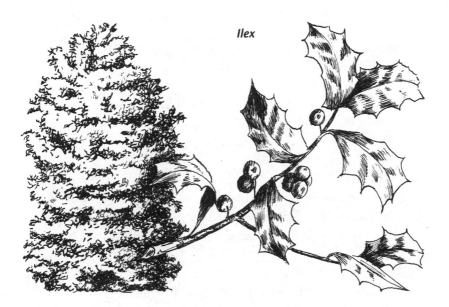

Ilex

Ilex
The botanical name for holly.

imbricate
A term used to describe leaves or petals that are overlapping, like shingles.

immortelle
The French word for everlasting. *See also* **everlasting**.

inbred seed
Seed produced when a bisexual plant pollinates itself.

incanus, -a, -um
As a species name, means "hoary or gray." Usually plants look gray because the leaves and stems are covered with short white hairs, as is the case, for example, with horehound, *Marrubium incanum*.

incise
To make a cut in a leaf or stem before grafting.

indefinite
A term used to describe a flower with a great many petals, too many to count, or an inflorescence with too many florets to count.

indehiscent
A term used to describe fruits that do not open or split to release their seeds, or anthers that do not open to discharge pollen. The hazelnut is an example of an indehiscent fruit.

indeterminate
A term used to describe a plant whose stems can continue to grow after flowering starts. The distinction between indeterminate and determinate is most often used in connection with vegetables. Indeterminate tomatoes and runner beans, for example, keep setting fruit until killed by the cold. *See also* **determinate**.

indicus, -a, -um
As a species name, literally means "from India," but like other terms of geographic origin, can refer to plants that grow throughout southeastern Asia. For example, crape myrtle, *Lagerstroemia indica,* is native to China.

indigenous
Native to an area.

indumentum
The coating of fine hairs on the underside of some leaves, such as those of some magnolias and rhododendrons.

infertile
A term usually used to describe soils lacking in nutrients.

inflorescence

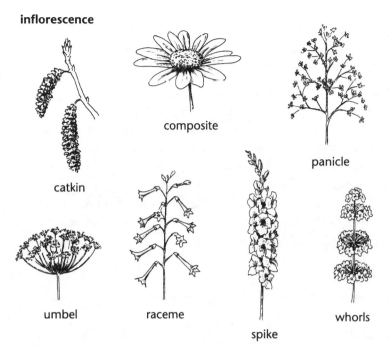

catkin

composite

panicle

umbel   raceme

spike

whorls

inflorescence
A cluster of flowers arranged in a particular way on a stem. Spikes, racemes, umbels, whorls, panicles, cymes, and corymbs are common types of inflorescences.

infundibular
Funnel shaped, like the flower of the morning glory.

inorganic fertilizer
A chemical product, of either mineral or synthetic origin, that provides nutrients to stimulate plant growth.

insecticidal soap
A particular kind of soap that is mixed with water and used as an insecticidal spray, as an alternative to more-toxic chemical controls.

insecticide
Any substance used to kill insects.

insectivorous plant
See carnivorous plant.

Integrated Pest Management (IPM)
A system of pest control that takes into consideration all aspects of the garden ecosystem, rather than focusing on a pest as an isolated nuisance to be eliminated. It relies on regular monitoring of the pest population to determine if and when to take action. When control is warranted, nontoxic strategies — traps, mulch, beneficial insects — are employed first. Then, if necessary, natural or synthetic pesticides may be employed as a last resort.

integument
The coating of an ovule that becomes the skin of a seed.

intercropping
Planting rows of fast-maturing plants, such as radishes, between rows of slower-growing ones. *See also* interplant.

intergeneric cross
A very rare type of hybrid formed between plants of two different genera. It is indicated by the symbol × before the genus name. For example, the Leyland cypress, × *Cupressocyparis leylandii,* is a cross between *Cupressus macrocarpa* and *Chamaecyparis nootkatensis.*

internode
The section of stem between two adjacent nodes.

interplant
To combine plants with different bloom times or growth habits. This makes it possible to fit more plants in a single bed and prolongs the season of interest. *See also* intercropping.

interrupted
A rarely used term describing an inflorescence having flowers unevenly distributed along the axis, with conspicuous gaps.

interspecific cross
A hybrid between two species.

intraspecific cross
A hybrid between plants of the same species.

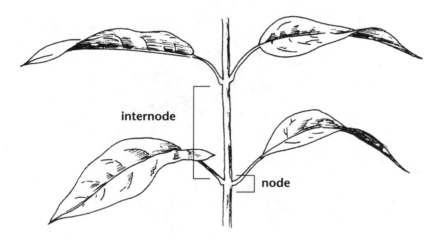

invasive
A term used to describe a plant that spreads aggressively, often by runners or other underground parts, and can overwhelm adjacent plantings. Many ground covers can be invasive.

involucre
One or more whorls of small leaves or bracts, typically green, arranged directly underneath a flower or flower head. Many composite flowers such as zinnias and strawflowers have involucral bracts.

IPM
See **Integrated Pest Management.**

involucre

Ipomoea
The botanical name for morning glory.

iron
A nutrient needed for the manufacture of chlorophyll. Plants in alkaline soils may not be able to absorb iron, resulting in chlorosis of their leaves.

iron chelate
A form of iron that can be absorbed by plants. Often added to alkaline soils, especially where gardeners want to grow rhododendrons, hollies, or other acid-loving plants.

irregular flower
A flower with petals that are not uniform in size or shape. For example, mint, ajuga, and larkspur bear irregular flowers. *See also* **zygomorphic**.

island bed
See **bed**.

Japanese beetle

A destructive beetle, *Popillia japonica,* whose larvae — fat
white grubs — eat the roots of grass and other plants. The
adults eat the flowers and skeletonize the leaves of roses
and many other plants.

Japanese garden

A garden that seeks to re-create nature on a small garden-
sized scale. Through its maker's choice and placement of
plants, it is meant to suggest the wildness of nature, a sense
of motion, and the passage of time. Japanese gardens
usually incorporate Shinto or Zen elements as well.

japonicus, -a, -um

As a species name, means "native to Japan" but is also
used for plants from that general area. For example, the
Japanese maple, *Acer japonicum,* and scores of other
garden plants have been introduced from Japan.

jardiniere

An ornamental container for displaying plants. According
to Norman Taylor in his *Taylor's Encyclopedia of
Gardening,* "jardiniere" is a "thoroughly misleading term,
for it is from the French for 'gardener,' while most
jardinieres work mischief to potted plants" because they

are made of airtight and watertight material and do not
allow for the air or drainage needed by plant roots.

Jekyll, Gertrude (1843–1932)
(Pronounced Gee'kill.) English garden designer, as famous
today as in her own time in England. She set gardens free
of the Victorian stylized geometrically patterned beds in
favor of long borders planted in magnificent "drifts"—her
word—of color. Of her 14 books, she is best known today
for *Colour in the Garden*. She is credited with designing or
influencing more than 300 gardens in addition to her own
garden at Munstead Wood.

Jensen, Jens (1860–1951)
Landscape architect who emigrated from Denmark to
Chicago in the late 1800s and is the father of today's
Prairie Style of landscaping. Along with Thomas Church,
he was one of the first landscape architects to promote the
use of native plants, in his case the prairie grasses and
plants of his adopted midwestern region.

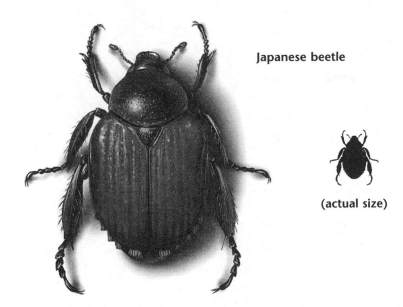

Japanese beetle

(actual size)

Juniperus

John Innes composts
In England, various potting soils formulated by the John Innes Horticultural Institute.

June drop
The normal early dropping of some of the immature fruits of the apple or other fruit trees.

Juniperus
The botanical name for juniper.

juvenile foliage

Distinct forms of leaves present only on young plants or
new growth. In many junipers, as shown below, the
juvenile foliage is needlelike, while the adult leaves are
flattened like scales.

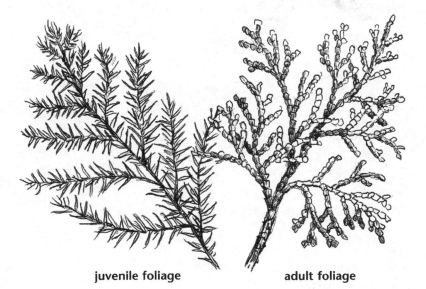

juvenile foliage   adult foliage

K
The chemical symbol for potassium. Used in the formula
NPK of a complete fertilizer.

Kalmia
The botanical name for mountain laurel.

keel
A sharp ridge or rib on the underside of a petal, leaf, or
other plant part.

Kalmia

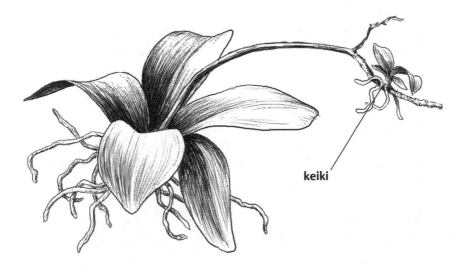

keiki

keiki
In orchids, a plantlet that develops from a node on the stem or cane.

Keukenhof
A showcase park created by bulb growers in the Netherlands.

Kew Gardens
The Royal Botanic Gardens, located on the River Thames in southwest London. It dates back to 1759, when the mother of King George III laid out a portion of her estate for a collection of plants assembled primarily for scientific and educational purposes. Today it also includes many ornamental displays.

key
See **samara**.

kitchen garden
A plot or garden planted with vegetables and herbs used in cooking, located near the house. Generally more decorative than an ordinary vegetable garden, it may also include flowers.

knot garden
A formal garden bed of small compact shrubs or herbs, planted in an intricate, intertwining pattern and kept neat by frequent shearing.

Koelreuteria
The botanical name for golden-rain tree.

Kolkwitzia
The botanical name for beautybush.

koreanus, -a, -um
As a species name, means "native to Korea" but is also used for plants from that general area. The Korean fir, *Abies koreana,* is one example. Many new plants have been introduced from Korea in recent years. Most are beautiful and hardy, but nurseries have not yet had time to propagate enough of them for widespread distribution.

labellum

Lip. Usually used to refer to the third petal of an orchid flower, modified by evolution into a lip that often serves as an attractive landing platform for pollinators.

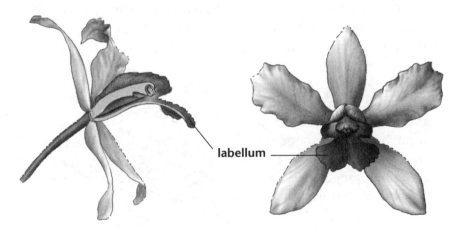

labellum

labiate

With flower parts arranged into two lips. Mints, thymes, salvias, and other members of Labiatae, the mint family, have labiate flowers.

lacewing

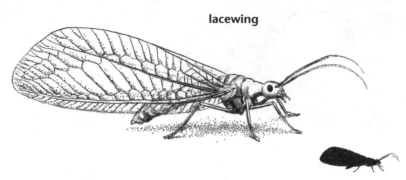

(actual size)

lacewing
A beneficial insect whose larvae eat aphids, mites, and thrips.

lact-
As part of a Latin name, means "milky." For example, white mugwort, *Artemisia lactiflora,* has milky white flowers. Lettuce, *Lactuca sativa,* has milky sap.

ladybug
A brightly colored beetle that eats aphids, gnats, mealybugs, and other small insects. Not all ladybugs have the orange bodies with black dots that we generally associate with the breed, but they are all beneficial insects. Their larvae are also predatory.

ladybug

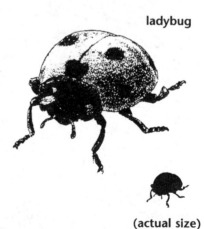

(actual size)

Lagerstroemia
The botanical name for crape myrtle.

Lamium
The botanical name for dead nettle.

lanceolate
Shaped like a lance; several times longer than wide, pointed at the tip and broadest near the base. Usually refers to leaves.

landscape architect
A professional, licensed in most states, who is trained to design solutions for all kinds of landscaping situations, including jobs that require earth-moving, drainage, or major construction work as well as choosing which plants to grow.

landscape contractor
Someone who supervises the creation of a new landscape, including construction, soil preparation, and planting,

Lamium

usually in accordance with plans drawn up by a garden designer or landscape architect.

landscape designer
See garden designer.

landscape fabric
A porous material made from paper, plastic, or synthetic fibers, sold by the roll and used as a weed barrier. It is often topped with a layer of bark chips or gravel, to disguise it.

landscape timber
A used railroad tie or similarly shaped piece of wood used to edge beds, make steps, or build retaining walls. It typically measures at least 4 inches by 4 inches in cross section and 8 feet or longer.

language of flowers
A "language" devised by illiterate women in the Ottoman seraglios to take the place of written language, which was forbidden them. It was described with scorn by Lady Mary Wortley Montagu in her letters from Turkey but was later all the rage among European women.

Larix
The botanical name for larch.

lateral
Attached to or at the side; a bud borne in the axil of a leaf or a branch but not at its tip.

lath house
A structure covered with narrow wooden slats that let air and light through the roof while screening plants from the hot sun and dry winds.

Lavandula

latifolius, -a, -um
As a species name, means "with broad (or broader than average) leaves." For example, northern sea oats, *Chasmanthium latifolium,* has leaf blades up to ³/₄ inch wide, which is greater than the blade width of many other grasses.

Latin names
See botanical Latin.

Laurus
The botanical name for laurel.

Lavandula
The botanical name for lavender.

Lavatera
The botanical name for tree mallow.

lawn
An area of ground planted with grass that is kept low by mowing.

lax
A term used to describe growth or habit that is loose or floppy.

layering
Starting a new plant by fastening a stem down to the ground and partially covering it with soil to induce roots to develop. The rooted stem can later be removed and planted separately. *See also* **air layering**.

leaching
The loss of nutrients when rain or irrigation carries them down through the soil and out of the root zone.

leader
The central upward-growing stem of a single-trunked tree.

leaf
A usually green, flattened structure attached to the stem that functions as the principal organ of photosynthesis and transpiration in most plants.

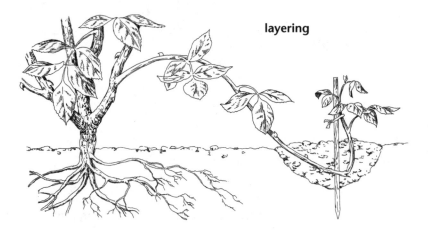

layering

leader

leaf cutting
A means of propagating certain tropical plants, including begonias, African violets, and gloxinias.

leaf hopper
Any of numerous insects of the family Cicadellidae that suck juices from plants.

leaflet
One of the subdivisions of a compound leaf.

leaf margin
The edge of a leaf.

leaf miner
Any of numerous small flies and moths that in the larval stage tunnel through and feed on leaf tissue.

leaf mold
Partially decayed or composted leaves.

leaf roller
Any of several moths whose larvae make nests of rolled leaves and silk.

leaf scar
The mark left on a twig after a leaf falls.

leaf spot
Any of various fungal or bacterial diseases that result in a well-defined necrotic spot on a leaf. The roundish spots may be of various colors.

leggy
A term usually used to describe perennials or shrubs that form tall stalks or shoots with sparse foliage on the bottom half. Also refers to seedlings or houseplants that have grown tall and thin because of insufficient light.

legume
A member of the legume or pea family (Leguminosae, formerly Fabaceae), a group that includes clovers, beans, wisteria, and mimosa.

Leguminosae
The legume or pea family, formerly called Fabaceae. It is a large family of about 600 genera and 12,000 species.

Le Nôtre, André (1613–1700)
The foremost French Renaissance garden designer. He designed the gardens of Versailles.

lenticel
A breathing pore in the young bark of a woody stem.
Cherry trees, for example, have conspicuous lenticels.

Leopold, Aldo (1886–1948)
Considered the prophet of the conservation movement and
a pioneer whose *A Sand County Almanac* became its bible.
His viewpoint is encapsulated in his land ethic, "that the
concept of community be expanded to include soils, waters,
plants, and animals, or, collectively: the land." As founding
director of the University of Wisconsin Arboretum, he
helped create the discipline of restoration ecology.

Leptospermum
The botanical name for tea tree.

leuc-
As part of a Latin name, means "white." For example,
pincushion, *Leucospermum,* has white flowers.

Leucojum
The botanical name for snowflake.

Liatris
The botanical name
for gayfeather or
blazing star.

Liatris

Lilium

lichen
A composite organism formed by the symbiotic association of a fungus and an alga. Lichens form small patches of crusty, leaflike, or branching growth; in many shades of green, gray, brown, orange, and other colors; on tree trunks, rocks, and soil. They are especially abundant in humid climates.

light shade
An area that receives full shade for a few hours during the hottest part of the day, or one that receives some sun and some shade throughout the day.

light soil
Sandy soil that dries out rapidly. Compared with heavy clay soil, it is lighter in weight and lighter in color.

ligneous
Woody.

lignin
A compound that binds to cellulose fibers and strengthens the cell walls of plants. It gives stiffness to stems and stalks.

Ligustrum
The botanical name for privet.

Liliaceae
The lily family, with about 240 genera and 3,000 species. It includes medicinal plants such as the aloe, edible plants like the onion, and, of course, the garden lily, among other ornamental bulbs.

Lilium
The botanical name for lily.

limb
A main branch of a tree or shrub.

limbing up
Removing the lower limbs of large trees to open space and to allow light and air to reach lower plants.

lime, limestone
White mineral compounds used to combat soil acidity and to supply calcium for plant growth. Quicklime is calcium oxide; slaked lime is calcium hydroxide; limestone is calcium carbonate.

Limonium
The botanical name for sea lavender.

Linaria
The botanical name for toadflax.

Linnaeus, Carolus (1707–1778)
Perhaps the most famous botanist of all time. While commonly called Linnaeus, he was a Swede whose real name was Karl von Linné. His great contribution was to devise the binomial system for naming plants that is still

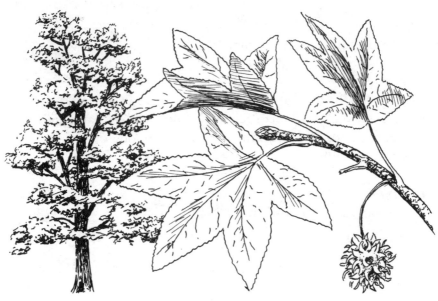

Liquidambar

used today. He gave every plant only two names, the first for its genus and the second for its species. *Aster,* for instance, is the genus of a group of plants that have many characteristics in common and are closely related. But with more than 250 different asters in this genus, the only way you can tell one from the other is to know what species it is. The specific epithet, or species name, further describes the plant by its characteristics or by who discovered it or where it grows. Linnaeus used the international language of educated people, Latin. Thus *Aster alpinus* is the name of a rock-garden plant from the mountains. *Aster novae-angliae* is the New England aster.

The great advantage of the Linnaean system is that no two species of plants in the world have the same name. This eliminates the confusion that is often caused by using common names, since the same plant may have more than one common name, and the same common name may be used for different plants. For example, the vine *Solanum dulcamara* is usually called nightshade but is also called bittersweet. On the other hand, the vines best known as bittersweet are not *Solanum* at all but *Celastrus orbiculatus* (Oriental bittersweet) and *Celastrus scandens* (American bittersweet). *See also* **botanical Latin.**

Linum
The botanical name for flax.

lip
See **labellum.**

Liquidambar
The botanical name for sweet gum.

Liriodendron
The botanical name for tulip tree.

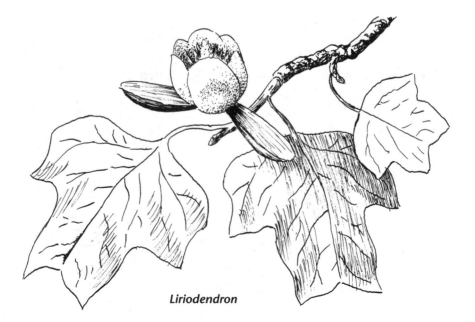

Liriodendron

Liriope
The botanical name for lilyturf.

Liriope

lithophyte
A plant that grows on rock and derives its nourishment chiefly from the atmosphere. For example, lichens and some orchids are lithophytes.

loam
An ideal soil for gardening, composed of moderate amounts of sand, silt, and clay. Loam soils are easy to till and effective in retaining moisture and nutrients.

lobe
A segment of a cleft leaf or petal.

lobed
A term used to describe a leaf whose margin is divided into broad rounded segments. *See also* **dissected; toothed.**

Lobularia
The botanical name for sweet alyssum.

Lobularia

Lonicera

loess
Wind-deposited, usually very rich fine soils, covering many states in the central part of the United States. They vary from fine, siltlike material to soils that are similar to rich garden loam.

long-day plant
A plant whose flowering is triggered by long hours of daylight or artificial light. *See also* **photoperiodism**.

Longwood Gardens
The former du Pont estate, located 30 miles west of Philadelphia, which is one of the outstanding public gardens in the United States. Of its 1,000 acres, 350 are devoted to outdoor gardens and 3½ acres are under glass in its spectacular conservatories. Another 20 greenhouses are open to the public.

Lonicera
The botanical name for honeysuckle.

loppers
See **lopping shears.**

lopping shears
Long-handled pruners designed to cut branches too thick for hand pruners and too small to require a pruning saw, and to cut out roots. Also called loppers.

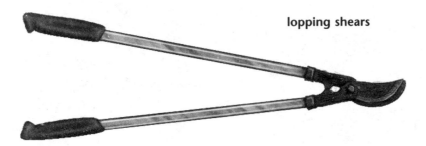

lopping shears

Los Angeles State and County Arboretum
A 127-acre garden that includes many educational demonstration plots of plants that grow well in southern California.

lucens or *lucidus, -a, -um*
As a species name, means "bright, shining, or clear." For example, glossy privet, *Ligustrum lucidum,* has very shiny leaves.

Lunaria
The botanical name for honesty or money plant.

Lupinus
The botanical name for lupine.

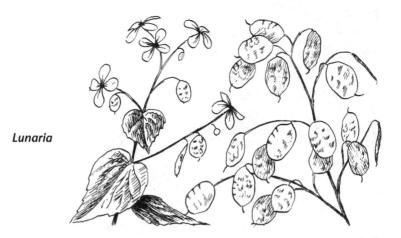

Lunaria

lute-

As part of a species name, means "yellow." For example, yellowwood, *Cladrastis lutea,* is a deciduous tree that really does have yellow wood.

Lychnis

The botanical name for catchfly or campion.

Lysimachia

The botanical name for loosestrife.

Lysimachia

macro-
As part of a species name, means "very large," or at least larger than average. For example, bigleaf magnolia, *Magnolia macrophylla,* has leaves up to 30 inches long.

macronutrients
The major elements essential for plant growth. Plants draw carbon, hydrogen, and oxygen from the air and from water. The principal other macronutrients, which they get from the soil, are nitrogen, phosphorus, and potassium, and to a lesser degree sulfur, calcium, and magnesium. *See also* **complete fertilizer; micronutrients; primary nutrients; secondary nutrients.**

maculatus, -a, -um
As a species name, means "spotted." For example, spotted dead nettle, *Lamium maculatum,* has green leaves marked with white or silver spots.

Mahonia
The botanical name for Oregon grape.

major nutrients
See **macronutrients.**

Malus

male
A plant having only staminate flowers.

Malmaison
The garden of Napoleon's empress Josephine, noted for its thousands of roses.

Malus
The botanical name for apple and crab apple.

Malva
The botanical name for mallow.

Malva

manure

Generally an animal manure, the most common source of nitrogen for composting. Cow, horse, and poultry manures are the most readily available. Dog and cat droppings may contain disease organisms that affect humans and should not be included in compost that may be used for food plants. *See also* **green manure.**

manure tea

A solution made by soaking manure in water. The resulting "tea" is used as a liquid fertilizer. *See also* **compost tea.**

Maranta

The botanical name for prayer plant.

margin

The border of a leaf.

marginal plant

A plant that grows on the margins of ponds or other bodies of water, in constantly damp soil or even in shallow water.

Marie Selby Botanical Garden

In Sarasota, Florida, a 7-acre garden featuring trees hung with epiphytic orchids and bromeliads, as well as a test garden with tropical fruits and vegetables.

marsh

Soft, wet, low-lying land characterized by herbaceous vegetation, often forming a transition between land and water.

marsh hay

See **salt marsh hay.**

Massachusetts Horticultural Association
An organization founded in 1829, and the sponsor of the annual New England Flower Show since 1871. It has a stunning horticultural library with many rare books.

mass planting
Filling an area with just one or a few kinds of plants spaced close together. Often done to create a bold dramatic effect or to reduce maintenance.

Matthiola
The botanical name for stock.

meadow garden
A mixed planting of herbaceous perennial plants, usually including grasses and native or naturalized wildflowers, maintained (once established) by annual mowing.

Matthiola

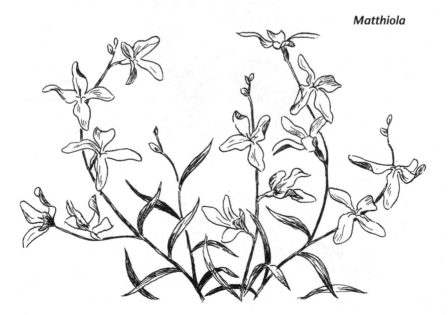

mealybug

A small, soft-bodied sucking insect whose body is covered with cottony tufts. Most kinds of mealybugs are white and feed on leaves or stems, but root mealybugs are gray and feed on roots and rootstocks, usually not far below the surface of the soil. Since they are killed by a hard frost, mealybugs are most troublesome on indoor or greenhouse plants and in warm regions.

mealybug

(actual size)

medium

Potting soil or other materials in which a container plant is grown. Also called growing medium.

medulla

Pith; the soft tissue in the center of young shoots and roots.

Melissa

Melissa
The botanical name for balm.

Mentha
The botanical name for mint.

mericlone
A generally exact copy of an original orchid plant made via the laboratory technique of meristem propagation.

meristem
An area of actively dividing cells found at the tips of shoots and roots and in the cambium.

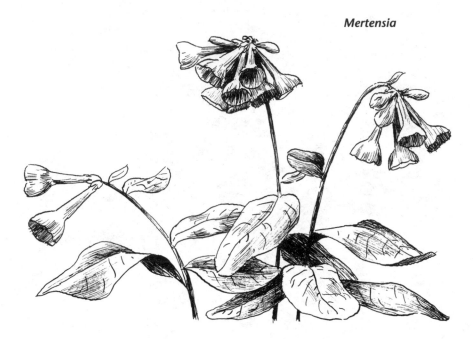

Mertensia

Mertensia
The botanical name for Virginia bluebells.

Metasequoia
The botanical name for dawn redwood.

Michaux, André (1746–1802)
French botanist who explored the Piedmont and mountain regions of the Carolinas and was the first to identify the native *Rhododendron catawbiense.*

micro-
As part of a species name, means "very small." For example, littleleaf boxwood, *Buxus microphylla,* has smaller leaves than other kinds of boxwoods do.

microclimate
Local conditions of shade, exposure, wind, drainage, and other factors that affect plant growth at any particular site. Gardeners take advantage of microclimates to grow plants that would otherwise not succeed in their general area.

micronutrients
Elements that are essential for plant growth but that are needed in very small quantities. Also called trace elements. These are iron, manganese, boron, copper, zinc, and molybdenum. *See also* **complete fertilizer; macronutrients**.

micropropagation
Making new plants by laboratory techniques, such as tissue culture, that start with microscopic pieces of the parent plant.

midrib
The primary rib or midvein of a leaf or leaflet.

mildew
Any of several fungi that form a superficial growth on plants. Mildew growth is stimulated by high humidity and poor air circulation.

Mimosa
The botanical name for sensitive plant.

Mimulus
The botanical name for monkey flower.

miniature
Like a dwarf, a plant that is small for its species. Generally, however, there are no set standards to distinguish these sizes.

mite

(actual size)

Minnesota State Horticultural Society
A major resource for northern gardeners, with 200
chapters, a bimonthly newsletter and several books, and
display gardens.

Missouri Botanical Garden
Established in 1859 in St. Louis, a major botanical research
center and the self-proclaimed oldest botanic garden in the
United States. Its Climatron, a geodesic dome conservatory
designed by Buckminster Fuller, is divided into four
separate climatic environments, with plants appropriate
to each.

mist system
A plumbing setup used in greenhouses to hasten the
development of cuttings by keeping the leaves moist
without soaking the soil.

mite
A virtually invisible spiderlike arachnid that sucks sap from leaves. Mites are especially troublesome in warm dry weather. Also called spider mite.

miticide
A pesticide that specifically kills spider mites and may or may not kill insects.

mitosis
Cell division in which the chromosomes are duplicated.

mixed border
A border that includes shrubs, bulbs, perennials, and annuals.

mold
Any of various fungi that attack plants.

mollis, -e
As a species name, means "soft or covered with soft hairs," like the leaves of lady's mantle, *Alchemilla mollis.*

Monarda
The botanical name for bee balm and bergamot.

Monarda

Monet
See **Giverny**.

monocarpic
A term used to describe a plant that flowers and fruits once and then dies. Annuals, for example, are monocarpic. More unusual are the so-called century plant, other agaves, and most bamboos, which can grow for years or decades before they suddenly flower and die.

monocot
The common shortened form of the term "monocotyledon."

monocotyledon
A plant having only one cotyledon and usually having parallel-veined leaves and flower parts arranged in groups of three. Common examples are grasses, bamboos, palms, lilies, daffodils, irises, hostas, and orchids. *See also* **dicotyledon**.

monoecious
Having separate male and female flowers but on the same plant. *See also* **dioecious**.

monopodial
One of two forms of orchid vegetative growth (the other is sympodial), wherein a single vegetative shoot grows continually upward without branching, such as the central rosette of *Phalaenopsis*. *See also* **sympodial**.

monopodial

montanus, -a, -um
As a species name, means "native to mountainous habitats." For example, mountain bluet (also called perennial bachelor's button), *Centaurea montana,* is native to the Alps.

Monticello
The home of Thomas Jefferson near Charlottesville, Virginia. The gardens he designed and documented in his "Garden Book" included a 1,000-foot-long vegetable plot. Much of the site has been restored according to his notes, and today the plantings feature both flowers and vegetables grown before 1826.

moon garden
A garden planted with white flowers, designed to be particularly effective at night.

moon gardening
Also called astrological gardening. A planting schedule based on the phases of the moon. Just as the moon's gravitational pull affects the tides, moon gardeners believe that this pull influences the liquids in plants. At its simplest (and it can be extremely detailed), this decrees planting aboveground food crops during the moon's first and second quarters, when the light is increasing. During the third and fourth quarters, when the light is decreasing, underground root crops should be planted.

morphology
The study of the form and structure of plants and animals.

Morton Arboretum
A Lisle, Illinois, institution that features more than 3,000 native and imported shrubs, vines, and trees that will grow in the Midwest.

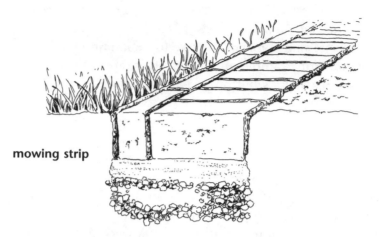

mowing strip

mosaic
A viral disease of plants, resulting in light and dark areas in the leaves, which often become shriveled and dwarfed. Infected plants cannot be cured and eventually die.

moss
Any of a group of small, flowerless, nonvascular plants, usually found in damp shady sites with acid soil.

moss pole
A device to support indoor climbing or vining plants. It usually consists of sphagnum moss attached to a flat piece of wood, but it may also be a wire cylinder filled with moss.

Mt. Auburn Cemetery
Founded in 1831 in Cambridge, Massachusetts, the oldest and arguably the most beautiful garden cemetery in America, with 2,500 identified trees, many of them more than 100 years old, on its grounds. With its hilly terrain, three lakes, and thousands of shrubs and landscaped flower beds, the cemetery attracts both human and avian visitors.

mowing strip
A flat level edging, usually of stone or brick, between a flower bed and the lawn, making it easy to mow the grass without damaging the plantings.

muck
Dark, heavy, fertile soil composed mostly of organic matter, either decayed plants or rotted manure. In England, "muck" refers to barnyard manure.

mulch
A layer of bark, peat moss, compost, shredded leaves, hay or straw, lawn clippings, gravel, paper, plastic, or other material spread over the soil around the base of plants. During the growing season, a mulch can help retard evaporation, inhibit weeds, and regulate soil temperature. In the winter, a mulch of evergreen boughs, coarse hay, or noncompacting leaves can help protect plants from heaving.

multiflora
A term used to describe roses or petunias that produce clusters of small flowers.

Munstead Wood
The private gardens of Gertrude Jekyll, in Surrey, England.

Muscari
The botanical name for grape hyacinth.

multiflora rose

mutant
An accidental variation in a plant, such as the formation of variegated leaves or double flowers. *See also* **sport**.

mycology
The study of fungi.

mycorrhiza (plural: **mycorrhizae**)
The common association formed between the mycelium of a fungus and the roots of certain plants, notably oaks, beeches, nearly all the heath family, and most orchids. The association is a symbiotic one, of advantage to both organisms. Plants that rely on mycorrhizae should be transplanted with some of their native soil if possible.

Myosotis
The botanical name for forget-me-not.

Myrica
The botanical name for myrtle and bayberry.

Myrica

N
The chemical symbol for nitrogen. Used in the formula NPK of a complete fertilizer.

naked
Unprotected by scales; lacking a perianth; without leaves.

Nandina
The botanical name for heavenly bamboo.

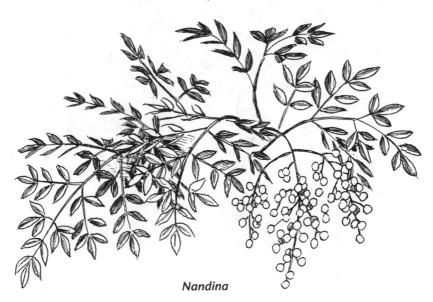

Nandina

nanus, -a, -um
As a species name, or more commonly a variety or cultivar name, means "dwarf." Frequently used for dwarf forms of conifers, such as the dwarf balsam fir, *Abies balsamea* 'Nana'.

Narcissus
The botanical name for daffodil, jonquil, and narcissus.

National Wildflower Research Center
Founded by Lady Bird Johnson, a young organization that has quickly become a leader in the field of wildflower protection and education. Its stunning new center, which opened in 1995, is in Austin, Texas.

native
A plant that grows naturally in a particular region and was not introduced from some other area.

Narcissus

Native Seeds/SEARCH
A nonprofit organization working to conserve traditional crops of the United States and northern Mexico, as well as their wild relatives.

natural gardening
A garden style that features plants native to the region; lets the plants develop their natural shape without pruning, staking, or shearing; and minimizes the use of pesticides and fertilizers.

naturalized
1. A term used to describe a plant that grows without assistance and reproduces in an area other than its native region. For example, many roadside wildflowers, such as oxeye daisy, *Leucanthemum vulgare,* are European natives that have naturalized in the United States.
2. A term used to describe garden plants such as daffodils that spread by themselves and persist for years with no human care or intervention.

necrosis
The death of plant tissue in small patches or zones, in response to disease, insect attack, or injury.

nectar
A very sweet substance, chiefly sugar and water, secreted by many flowers to attract pollinators.

nectary
A gland that contains nectar. It is usually located near the base of a petal or stamen. In the process of securing nectar, a pollinator becomes dusted with pollen, which is then transferred to the next flower it visits.

neem
A nontoxic botanical insecticide derived from the neem tree, *Azadirachta indica*.

Nelumbo
The botanical name for lotus.

nematode
A microscopic roundworm that lives in the soil. Some kinds of nematodes are beneficial and prey on harmful insect larvae, but many are serious pests that weaken plants by damaging their roots. Certain nematodes are also known as eelworms. *See also* **V,F,N**.

Nepeta
The botanical name for catmint.

Nephrolepis
The botanical name for sword fern.

Nelumbo

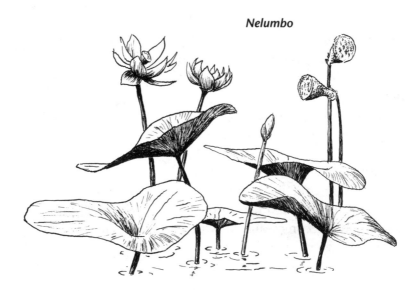

Nerium

Nerium
The botanical name for oleander.

neutral soil
Soil that is neither acid nor alkaline, having a pH of 7. *See also* **pH**.

New England Wild Flower Society
An organization with chapters in each New England state and a program of propagating and exchanging seeds with botanic gardens. Its Garden-in-the-Woods, located in Framingham, Massachusetts, contains the largest landscaped collection of northeastern native plants in the United States.

new wood
Stems or branches produced during the current growing season. *See also* **old wood**.

New York Botanical Garden (NYBG)
A 250-acre institution founded in 1891 by a Columbia University botanist who was inspired by the Royal Botanic Gardens at Kew. Located in the northern section of the Bronx, the NYBG comprises dramatic rock outcroppings, wetlands, ponds, a cascading waterfall, and a 40-acre tract of uncut forest typical of that which once covered New York City. It also boasts the nation's most beautiful Victorian glasshouse, the Enid A. Haupt conservatory.

Nicotiana
The botanical name for tobacco.

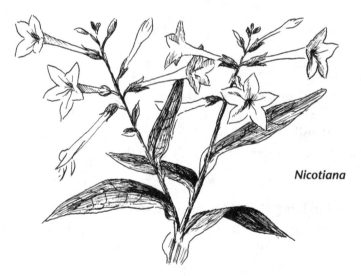

Nicotiana

Nigella
The botanical name for love-in-a-mist.

nigr-
As part of a species name, means "black or very dark green." For example, the Austrian pine, *Pinus nigra,* has very dark green needles.

nipponicus, -a, -um
As a species name, means "native to Japan." Many daisies, for example, are native to Eurasia, but the Nippon or Montauk daisy, *Chrysanthemum nipponicum* (now renamed *Nipponanthemum nipponicum*), came from Japan.

nitrogen
One of the three main nutrients in a complete fertilizer, designated by the chemical symbol N. Nitrogen is responsible primarily for vigorous growth and dark green leaves. *See also* **complete fertilizer.**

nitrogen-fixing bacteria
Particular kinds of bacteria that live in nodules on the roots of many plants in the legume family (Leguminosae) such as beans and clover, and some unrelated plants such as alder trees, and "fix" nitrogen from the air into a form that can be utilized by the host plants and, after these die, by plants that subsequently grow in that soil. *See also* **nodule.**

niv-
As part of a species name, refers to snow or to a snow-white color. For example, snowdrops, *Galanthus nivalis,* have white flowers and often bloom while there is still snow on the ground.

nocturnal
Having flowers that open at night.

node
A place on a stem where leaves or branches are attached. *See also* **internode.**

no-dig gardening
A method, first popularized by Ruth Stout in 1955 in her book *How to Have a Green Thumb Without an Aching*

Back, in which mulch is spread on beds and left in place to smother weeds and other unwanted vegetation. The garden is then planted through the mulch, which decomposes to enrich the soil. Each year, new mulch is added as a topdressing.

nodule
A small swelling on the roots of plants (mostly legumes) that contains bacteria able to absorb nitrogen from the air around the roots. Called nitrogen-fixing, these bacteria make the nitrogen available in a form that can be absorbed by the host plant. *See also* **nitrogen-fixing bacteria.**

nodules

North American Mycological Association
With 65 chapters, a group for mushroom growers and enthusiasts.

North Carolina Botanical Garden
Located in Chapel Hill, an institution with an outstanding collection of native southeastern plants, arranged by habitat. It is known for its research on the conservation and propagation of wildflowers and other native plants.

North Carolina State University Arboretum
(In 1997, renamed the J. C. Raulston Arboretum.) A small (8-acre) but very exciting garden in Raleigh, displaying several thousand species of trees, shrubs, and perennials

that are well adapted to the heat and humidity of the South. Many of these plants are new to American gardens and have been made available to nurseries for propagation through the arboretum's outreach program. *See also* **Raulston, J. C.**

NPK
The chemical symbols of the three major plant nutrients in a complete fertilizer: nitrogen (N), phosphorus (P), and potassium (K).

nucleus
The part of a cell that contains the chromosomes.

nursery
A place where young plants are propagated and grown until they are ready for permanent planting or for sale.

nursery bed
A bed that gardeners use to grow seedlings or transplants until they are ready to be planted in a permanent site.

nut
A large, hard, one-seeded fruit, such as an acorn or a walnut.

nutlet
A small nut, pit, or hard-coated seed. Grape seeds, for example, are sometimes called nutlets.

nutrients
Elements such as nitrogen and iron that are needed for plant growth. Nutrients released from the soil or supplied by fertilizer get dissolved in water and are absorbed by a plant's roots. *See also* **macronutrients; micronutrients.**

Nymphaea

Nymphaea
The botanical name for water lily.

Nyssa
The botanical name for tupelo, or sour gum tree.

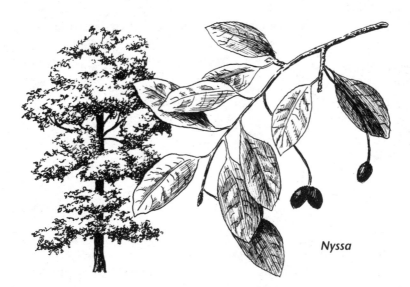

Nyssa

oblate
Spherical but slightly flattened at the top and bottom.

obtuse
Having a blunt or rounded tip.

occidentalis, -e
As a species name, means "western." Usually denotes a plant that is native to somewhere in the Western Hemisphere, such as American arborvitae, *Thuja occidentalis,* which is native to northeastern North America; but can denote a plant from the western United States, such as the western azalea, *Rhododendron occidentale,* native to Oregon and California.

occlusion
1. The closing over of a tree wound by formation of callus.
2. The plugging of the xylem by fungi such as verticillium, causing the plant to wilt.

Ocimum
The botanical name for basil.

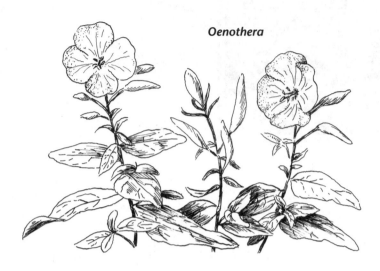

Oenothera

odor-
As part of a species name, means "fragrant." For example, sweet woodruff, *Galium odoratum,* has vanilla-scented foliage. Sweet violet, *Viola odorata,* has fragrant flowers.

Oenothera
The botanical name for evening primrose.

officinalis, -e
As a species name, denotes a plant that was traditionally sold in apothecary shops and was considered to have medicinal or healthful properties. For example, tea brewed from the leaves of garden sage, *Salvia officinalis,* was recommended for sore throats.

offset
A short lateral shoot arising near the base of a plant and readily producing new roots. Offsets can be detached and replanted away from the parent plant.

old wood
Stems or branches produced one or more years before the current growing season. *See also* **new wood**.

Olea
The botanical name for olive.

Olmsted, Frederick Law (1822–1903)
An illustrious 19th-century landscape designer, sometimes called the father of American landscape architecture, whose most memorable works are Central Park in New York City and the so-called Emerald Necklace, a string of parks or parkland in Boston. More than 80 parks in the United States bear his signature.

opacus, -a, -um
As a species name, means "dark or dull." For example, the American holly, *Ilex opaca,* typically has dark, even dull-looking olive green leaves. (However, cultivars have been selected that have brighter, glossier foliage.)

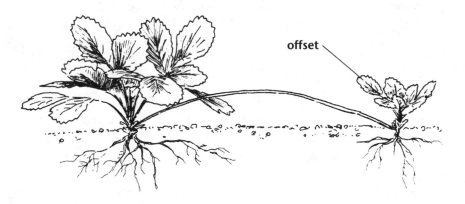

offset

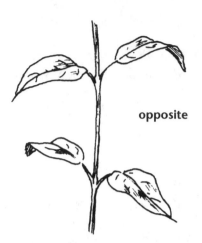

opposite

open-pollinated
A term used to describe varieties resulting from natural or uncontrolled pollination, as opposed to hybrids whose pollination is controlled.

opposite
A term used to describe parts such as leaves that are arranged in pairs along a stem or shoot. *See also* **alternate.**

orangery
A heated glasshouse, originally for growing citrus trees, that was a feature in grand 18th- and 19th-century English manor houses.

orchid
A plant of the family Orchidaceae, which is generally conceded to be the largest family of flowering plants, variously estimated as between 600 and 800 genera, with 17,000 to 30,000 species plus numerous hybrids.

organic
A term used to describe any material that contains carbon compounds and is derived from living or once-living plants or animals.

organic fertilizer

Technically, an animal or plant product or by-product used as fertilizer, such as manure, blood meal, alfalfa meal, seaweed, or compost. In practice, usually includes mineral-based fertilizers as well, such as greensand or rock phosphate. Organic fertilizers are now processed into a variety of granular and liquid forms. These products vary greatly in the amount and proportion of nutrients contained, and in the rate at which the nutrients are released into the soil.

organic gardening

A very old, and newly popular, concept in the proper management of the land. It involves growing plants without using synthetic fertilizers or pesticides, and the addition and preservation of humus, primarily by making and using a compost pile.

orchid

**ornamental
grass**

organic matter
Plant and animal residues such as leaves, trimmings, and manure in various stages of decomposition. *See also* **compost; humus**.

organism
A living plant, animal, fungus, or bacterium.

orientalis, -e
As a species name, means "from the Far East," often China. For example, Oriental poppy, *Papaver orientale,* comes from southwestern Asia.

orientation
The location or arrangement of a garden relative to the points of the compass.

ornamental
A common garden term for a plant cultivated primarily for its showy flowers or leaves, as opposed to a plant cultivated for food or other useful purposes.

ornamental grass

As opposed to a lawn grass, a grass that is not mown but is allowed to grow to its full potential and is used in the landscape in the same way as perennials or other ornamental plants.

Ornithogalum

The botanical name for star-of-Bethlehem.

Osmunda

The botanical name for flowering fern.

ovary

The ovule-bearing part of a pistil that develops into a fruit.

ovate

Oval, with the broader end at the base.

overpotting

Growing a plant in a pot that is too large for its root system, presumably in the hope that it will not be necessary to transplant. The more likely result is that the roots will rot.

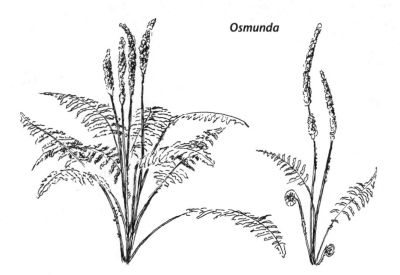

Osmunda

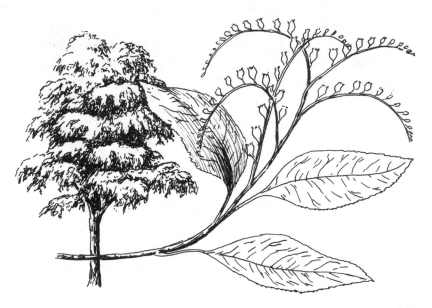

Oxydendrum

overseeding
Sowing seeds where other plants are already growing without first clearing and cultivating the ground. Usually refers to lawns, but also to cover crops in vegetable gardens.

ovule
A group of cells within the ovary that develops into a seed after fertilization.

oxalic acid
A sour-tasting compound in the leaves of some plants, such as rhubarb and sorrel. Ingestion can cause nausea or serious poisoning.

Oxalis
The botanical name for wood sorrel.

Oxydendrum
The botanical name for sourwood.

oxygenator
A submerged aquatic plant that releases oxygen into the water. Oxygenators are a necessity for water gardens and fish ponds.

P
The chemical symbol for phosphorus. Used in the formula
NPK of a complete fertilizer.

Paeonia
The botanical name for peony.

pallidus, -a, -um
As a species name, means "pale." Usually refers to pastel
flowers, as in pale purple coneflower, *Echinacea pallida*.

palm

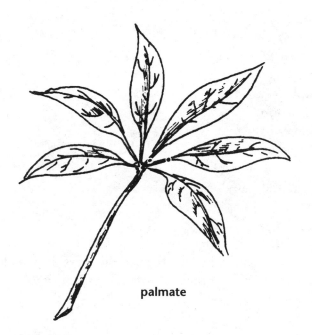

palmate

palm
A tropical shrub or tree of the family Palmaceae.

palmate
Having veins or leaflets arranged like the fingers on a hand, radiating out from a center point.

palmatus, -a, -um
As a species name, means "having palmate leaves," as on the running bamboo *Sasa palmata.*

palustris, -e
As a species name, means "native to swamps or marshes." For example, the swamp rose, *Rosa palustris,* is one of the few roses that thrive in poorly drained soil.

panicle
A loose, open, branching cluster of flowers that bloom from the center or bottom toward the edges or top. Examples of plants that produce panicles are yucca, catalpa, and baby's breath.

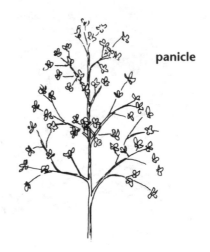

panicle

paniculatus, -a, -um
As a species name, means "bearing flowers in panicles," as in perennial baby's breath, *Gypsophila paniculata*.

Panicum
The botanical name for panic grass or switch grass.

Papaver
The botanical name for poppy.

papilla (plural: **papillae**)
A pimplelike projection on the surface of a petal or leaf. Many vines have papillae on the petals.

parasite
A plant that steals all its food from another, to which it is attached and which it typically injures. Tree-perching plants such as orchids and bromeliads are often mistakenly called parasites; they are actually epiphytes. Mistletoe, witch grass, and dodder are parasites, as are many fungi.

parterre
A geometric arrangement of ornamental garden beds
separated by a pattern of walks or grass paths. Parterres
are most effective if they can be viewed from above. As the
name implies, parterres were originally a French garden
design.

parthenocarpic
A term used to describe a plant that can develop fruit
without fertilization. Some examples are pineapples, naval
oranges, and bananas.

Parthenocissus
The botanical name for Virginia creeper and Boston ivy.

part shade
See **half shade.**

part sun
See **half shade.**

parvi-
As part of a species name, means "small." For example,
bottlebrush buckeye, *Aesculus parviflora,* has spikes of
small white flowers.

Passiflora
The botanical name for passionflower.

patens or *patulus, -a, -um*
As a species name, means "spreading." For example,
firebush, *Hamelia patens,* and 'Miss Kim' lilac, *Syringa
patula,* are both spreading shrubs that grow wider than tall.

pathogen
An organism, usually microscopic, that causes disease.

patio
An outdoor space for dining and recreation that adjoins a building and is often paved; a roofless inner courtyard typically found in Spanish or Spanish-style dwellings.

pea gravel
Round gravel about the size of peas, often used for paths or driveways.

peat moss
Partially decomposed mosses and sedges, mined from boggy areas and used to improve garden soil or to prepare potting soil. Most peat moss is sphagnum moss, a coarse-textured moss that grows in shallow freshwater bogs throughout the northern United States, Canada, and Europe. Peat from sphagnum moss is also known as sphagnum peat. Peat from natural deposits of decomposed reeds, sedges, cattails, and similar marsh plants is known as reed-sedge peat. Much less expensive than sphagnum peat, reed-sedge peat is coarse textured when young. However, it quickly breaks down into a fine-textured humus. Although a good conditioner when mixed with soil, peat moss should never be used as a mulch, because when it is dry, it forms a water-repellent crust that keeps rain or irrigation water from soaking into the soil.

peat pot
A pot for starting seeds, made from compressed peat. The entire pot can be planted and the roots of the seedling will grow through the walls of the pot, thus reducing any setback from transplanting.

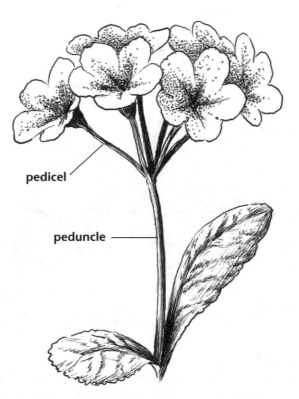

pectin
A substance in cell walls that binds cells together.

pedicel
The stalk of an individual flower in an inflorescence or cluster.

peduncle
The stalk of a solitary flower; the main stalk of a flower cluster. Each of the flowers in a cluster may have its own individual stalk, or pedicel.

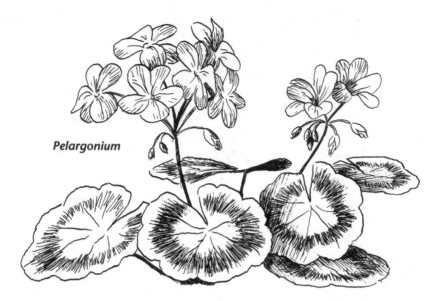

Pelargonium

Pelargonium
The botanical name for geranium.

pelleted seed
A seed enclosed in a pellet of inert material, which makes such seeds easier to handle. Pelleted seeds can be spaced more easily, reducing the need for thinning.

peltate
Having the stalk attached away from the margin of a leaf, and often in the center of it. Water lilies and nasturtiums are examples of plants with peltate leaves.

pend-
As part of a species name, means "drooping." For example, the European white birch, *Betula pendula,* has drooping twigs.

pendent
Drooping; hanging.

penjing
The Chinese art of dwarfing trees and shrubs, similar to Japanese bonsai.

Pennsylvania Horticultural Society
An extremely active society, with a 14,000-volume horticultural library. It offers lectures and workshops; publishes the magazine *Green Scene;* and sponsors the Philadelphia Flower Show, America's largest.

Penstemon
The botanical name for beard-tongue.

perennial
A plant that lives for a number of years, generally flowering each year. Gardeners often use the term "perennial" to mean herbaceous perennial, but woody plants such as shrubs and trees are also perennial. *See also* **short-lived perennial; herbaceous perennial; woody perennial.**

Penstemon

perennial border
A border filled primarily with herbaceous perennial plants.

Perennial Plant Association
An organization of nurseries that produce perennial plants.
It hosts an annual convention and names the Perennial
Plant of the Year, an honor that has been bestowed on
'Moonbeam' coreopsis, 'Sprite' astilbe, and other
noteworthy plants.

perennis, -e
As a species name, means "perennial." For example, *Linum
perenne* is a perennial flax with lovely blue flowers.

perfect flower
A flower that has both male and female parts, as opposed
to one that is unisexual or sterile.

perfoliate
A term used to describe a leaf or pair of leaves that encircle
a stem, as, for example, the juvenile foliage of silver-dollar
eucalyptus, *Eucalyptus cinerea*.

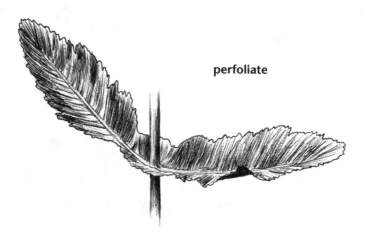

perfoliate

pergola
An arbor or passageway of columns supporting a roof of trelliswork on which climbing plants are trained to grow.

perianth
Collectively, all the sepals and petals of a flower.

perlite
A white, glasslike, volcanic mineral, about one-tenth the weight of sand, that is useful as a medium for rooting cuttings but lacks any nutrients. Perlite is also often added to soilless potting mixes.

permaculture
An agricultural system based on perennial plants, both herbaceous and woody, rather than on the annuals that now provide almost all of our food. To date, this is a visionary idea, not a reality. *See also* **sustainable agriculture.**

perpetual
A plant that is in bloom more or less continuously, such as the tropical hibiscus, *Hibiscus rosa-sinensis.*

persicus, -a, -um
As a species name, means "native to Persia." For example, the peach, *Prunus persica,* was domesticated in Persia (now Iran) or Central Asia.

persistent
1. Lasting past maturity without falling off, as the calyx on an eggplant or the scales of a pinecone.
2. A term used to describe a pesticide that remains effective (sometimes dangerously so) for a long time after it is applied.

pest
Any insect or other creature that damages plants. Strictly
speaking, bacteria and viruses are diseases, not pests,
although in practical terms, these — and also weeds — are
considered by gardeners to be pests.

pesticide
A general term for any compound used to kill insects,
mites, weeds, fungi, bacteria, or other pests.

petal
One of a series of flower parts, often brightly colored and
sometimes patterned.

petiole

petiole
The stalk of a leaf.

Petroselinum
The botanical name for parsley.

pH
A measure of the hydrogen ion content of a substance, and
thus a means of expressing the acidity or alkalinity of
garden soil, soilless mixes, rain or irrigation water, fertilizer
solutions, or pond water. *See also* **pH scale.**

Phalaenopsis
The botanical name for moth orchid.

phenology
The scientific study of periodic biological phenomena, such
as the flowering of plants, in relation to climatic conditions.

Gardeners use this study of regularly occurring cycles to judge planting dates. For example, in the Northeast the accepted wisdom is that the time to plant corn is when oak leaves are the size of a mouse's ear (and that same corn should be knee-high by the Fourth of July).

pheromone
A chemical released by an animal, particularly an insect, to communicate with other members of the same species. Synthetic pheromones are used to lure insects into traps or to disrupt mating habits.

Philadelphus
The botanical name for mock orange.

phloem
The food-conducting tissue of plants. *See also* **xylem.**

Phlomis
The botanical name for Jerusalem sage.

Philadelphus

Phormium
The botanical name for New Zealand flax.

phosphorus
One of the three main nutrients in a complete fertilizer, designated by the chemical symbol P. Phosphorus is responsible primarily for the development of roots, flowers, and seeds. *See also* **complete fertilizer.**

photoperiod
See **daylength.**

photoperiodism
The response of plants to the length of the day, especially as it affects their blooming. In temperate zones, long-day plants typically bloom in spring and early summer, short-day plants in fall. By manipulating light in greenhouses, growers can induce plants to bloom out of their seasons. Many plants are day-neutral, or not affected by the length of the day.

photosynthesis
As the etymology of the word suggests, an activity carried on in the light. It is the most important function of leaves. Powered by the energy from light, chlorophyll (the green pigment in leaves) combines carbon dioxide from the air with water, releasing oxygen and producing glucose sugar, the basic building block of plants.

phototropism
The tendency of shoots and leaves to grow toward the light. Also called heliotropism.

pH scale
A system of describing acidity or alkalinity, ranging from pH 0 to pH 14, with pH 7 being neutral. Values lower

than 7 indicate acidity; those higher than 7 indicate alkalinity. Each number on the pH scale represents a tenfold change in acidity or alkalinity. Thus pH 5 is 10 times more acid than pH 6, and pH 4 is 100 times more acid than pH 6; pH 11 is 1,000 times more alkaline than pH 8. In general, plants grow best in the pH range of 4 (very acid) to 8 (slightly alkaline).

The availability of nutrients to plants is directly correlated to the pH of the soil. Most of the essential elements are available in adequate quantities at pH levels from 5.8 to 7.

Phyllostachys
The botanical name for a genus of bamboo. *See also Bambusa.*

-phyllus, -a, -um
As part of a species name, refers to the leaves. For example, lemon verbena, *Aloysia triphylla,* has leaves arranged in groups of three.

phylum
The first level of division in the plant kingdom. Subdivisions, in descending rank, are class, order, family, genus, and species.

Physostegia
The botanical name for obedient plant.

Physostegia

pinching

phyto-
A prefix meaning "plant."

phytochrome
A pigment in plants that senses daylength and plays a role in controlling flowering, dormancy, and seed germination. *See also* **photoperiodism.**

phytogeography
The study of the distribution of plants.

Picea
The botanical name for spruce.

Pieris
The botanical name for andromeda.

pileus
The cap of a mushroom or toadstool.

pinching
Removing the top or central growing point of a plant to promote the development of side shoots. *See also* **apical dominance.**

pinetum
An arboretum or collection of conifers.

pinnate
Like a feather. Refers to compound leaves or fronds arranged in two rows on either side of a central stalk.

Pinus
The botanical name for pine.

pioneer plants
The first species to colonize an area after the soil is disturbed by fire, flood, or earthquake or after a farm or garden is abandoned.

Pinus

pisifera

pip
An offset or individual rootstock of a plant used for
propagation purposes, especially of lily-of-the-valley.

pisifera
As a species name, means "bearing pealike seeds." For
example, the Sawara false cypress, *Chamaecyparis pisifera,*
is a conifer that bears rounded seeds in small cones.

Pistacia
The botanical name for pistachio.

pistil
The complete female organ of reproduction in flowers. The
typical pistil consists of a usually swollen base (the ovary)
containing the ovules (which will become the seeds after
fertilization), a shanklike stalk (the style), and a club-
shaped or variously divided tip (the stigma), which is often
sticky. The deposition of pollen on the latter begins the
process ending in fertilization.

pith
The soft spongelike tissue in the center of young stems and stalks.

plant
Any multicellular organism of the kingdom Plantae characteristically containing chloroplasts, having cellulose cell walls, lacking the power of locomotion, and reproducing by seeds or spores.

planter
A container in which to grow plants.

plantlet
A tiny plant that is produced on the leaves of certain plants such as the pickaback plant, *Tolmiea menziesii*. When plantlets fall off and take root, they become new plants.

plant lice
A British term for aphids.

plant lights
Fluorescent and other specialized bulbs used to grow seedlings and other plants indoors.

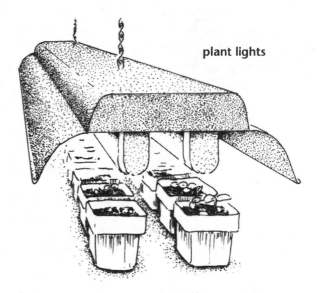

plant lights

Platanus

plant nutrients
See **macronutrients; micronutrients.**

plant society
An organization for gardeners who collect and grow a particular group of plants such as roses, conifers, or lilies. Plant societies are usually set up on a national scale, but they may have regional or local chapters. Most plant societies publish newsletters, run seed or cutting exchanges, maintain demonstration or research plots, and host annual conferences.

Platanus
The botanical name for sycamore or plane tree.

platy-
As part of a Latin name, means "broad" (not flat). For example, balloon flower, *Platycodon grandiflorus,* has broad, wide-open flowers.

Platycerium
The botanical name for staghorn fern.

pleaching
A method of pruning and training trees or shrubs to produce a hedgelike wall.

plicatus, -a, -um
As a species name, means "pleated." Usually refers to leaves. For example, double-file viburnum, *Viburnum plicatum* var. *tomentosum,* has leaves arranged on both sides of the branches, like a paper that is folded in half.

plug
A seedling or cutting grown in a special plastic tray that is divided into many small compartments, so it and its soil mass can be pushed out and planted without disturbing the roots.

plug

plum-
As part of a species name, means "feathery or fringed." For example, carnation, *Dianthus plumarius,* has fringed petals.

Plumbago
The botanical name for leadwort.

plunge

1. To bury a pot in which a houseplant is growing up to its rim in the garden, done in summer to refresh the plant. This is usually preferable to removing the plant from its pot, because the roots are still contained.
2. To water a potted plant by soaking it in a container of water deep enough to totally immerse the pot. This is a useful way to revive plants if the potting soil has gotten very dry.

Poaceae

See **Gramineae.**

poacher's spade

A spade with a narrow blade, useful for digging out a plant from a crowded flower bed without disturbing neighboring plants.

pod

A dry one-celled fruit with thicker walls than a capsule.

Polemonium

The botanical name for Jacob's ladder.

pole saw

A short pruning saw attached to a long handle, useful for pruning overhead branches.

pollard

To prune a tree so that all its main branches are cut back to the trunk. The result is a dense globelike mass of foliage.

pollen

Minute grains containing the male germ cells, produced in the anthers of flowers. Pollen is often yellow, but it comes in other colors, too. Examined under a microscope, pollen grains have very distinct shapes and surface textures. When a pollen grain is deposited on the stigma of a suitable flower, the germ cell travels down through the style and fuses with an ovule, which then grows into a seed.

pollination
The transfer of pollen from stamens to pistils, usually between two flowers on the same or different plants. *See also* **open-pollinated; self-pollination.**

pollinator
An agent that transfers pollen from one flower to another, accidentally or intentionally. Bees, butterflies, moths, other insects, hummingbirds, bats, and humans all serve as pollinators.

polyandrous
Having a large, indefinite number of stamens.

polygamous
Bearing both unisexual and perfect flowers on the same or different plants.

Polygonatum
The botanical name for Solomon's seal.

Polygonum
The botanical name for knotweed and silver fleece vine.

Polygonatum

Polypodiaceae
The polypody family, the largest family of ferns.

Polystichum
The botanical name for shield fern.

pome
Typically, the fruit of an apple, pear, quince, hawthorn, or related plant in the family Rosaceae, or rose family. Technically, it is a fleshy fruit enclosing several seeds.

pompon
A compact rounded flower head, typical on many types of chrysanthemums and dahlias.

Populus
The botanical name for cottonwood, poplar, and aspen.

postemergent weed killer
An herbicide that acts on weeds after they have sprouted.

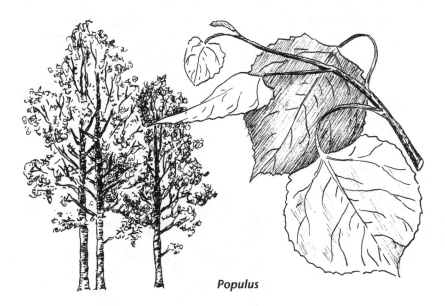

Populus

potager
A French-inspired vegetable garden laid out in a formal, ornamental style.

potash
Potassium. The word derives from the early method of leaching potassium from wood ashes and drying it in clay pots — in other words, pot ashes.

potassium
One of the three main nutrients in a complete fertilizer, designated by the chemical symbol K. Potassium is important in the development of flowers and fruits and helps to make sturdy plants resistant to wind, cold, drought, and other stresses. *See also* **complete fertilizer.**

pot-bound
A term used to describe a plant whose roots are confined by a relatively small pot, growing so closely that there seems to be no room for further growth. Some plants, however, bloom best when they are pot-bound.

Potentilla
The botanical name for cinquefoil.

potherb
An old-fashioned term for leaves of an herb, weed, or vegetable that, before serving, are traditionally boiled in a pot until they are very soft.

pot plant
See **houseplant.**

potpourri
A mixture of dried flowers, leaves, seeds, and spices used to scent a room.

potting on
Transplanting a plant into the next-size pot.

potting up
Transplanting seedlings or rooted cuttings from a flat into individual pots or containers.

powdery mildew
A fungal disease that typically produces a whitish or grayish residue on leaves. It is most common in summer when the soil is dry and the air is hot and humid. Lilacs and phlox are two plants commonly afflicted with powdery mildew.

praecox
As a species name, means "very early." For example, wintersweet, *Chimonanthus praecox,* blooms in late winter or very early spring.

prairie
A habitat dominated by perennial grasses and forbs, with few woody plants; particularly, the grasslands of the midwestern United States.

prairie gardening
A landscape style that features the native grasses and forbs of America's midwestern prairies. *See also* **Jensen, Jens.**

praying mantis
A large predatory insect that consumes aphids, caterpillars, and many other insect pests but also captures many beneficial insects.

precocious
Blossoming before the appearance of leaves.

predator
As used in horticulture, a "good-guy" insect that preys upon insects that eat plants. Predators include ladybugs and praying mantises.

preemergent weed killer
An herbicide that is applied before a plant emerges or before leaves sprout. Preemergents prevent seeds from germinating and growing and are used mostly to control annual weeds such as crabgrass.

pressure-treated lumber
Pine boards that have been treated with chemicals for protection from the fungi that cause untreated wood to decay or rot.

pricking out
A British term for transplanting tiny seedlings by holding the leaves and using a small utensil to loosen the roots so as not to damage either the stem or the roots.

pricking out

prickle
A small weak spine that grows out from a plant's bark or epidermis.

primary growth
Growth that results in the elongation of a stem or stalk, produced by cell divisions in the apical meristem. *See also* **secondary growth**.

primary nutrients
The macronutrients needed in the largest quantities by plants — namely, nitrogen (N), phosphorus (P), and potassium (K). *See also* **secondary nutrients; macronutrients; complete fertilizer**.

Primula
The botanical name for primrose.

procumbent
Prostrate; lying on the ground.

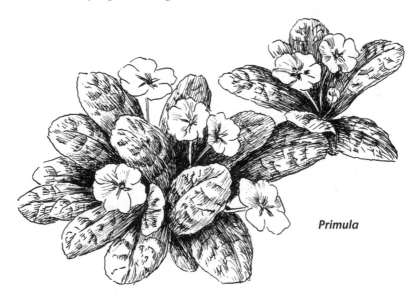

Primula

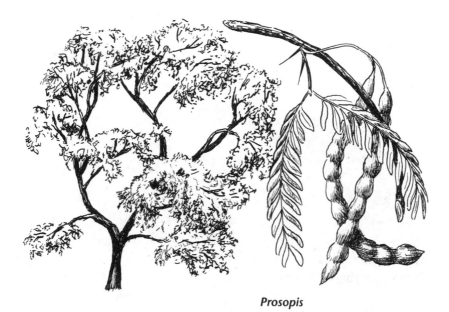

Prosopis

propagate
To produce new plants by sowing seeds, rooting cuttings, making divisions, layering, grafting, or other means.

propagule
An offset, bulbil, plantlet, or other naturally occurring portion of a plant, except seeds, from which a new plant may develop.

prop root
A root that acts as a prop or support. Prop roots originate from stems but ultimately penetrate the soil, serving both as anchors and as food gatherers. Corn and many tropical plants produce prop roots.

Prosopis
The botanical name for mesquite.

pruning saw

prostrate
Lying on the ground; creeping.

prune
To cut back, pinch back, or otherwise inhibit or control the growth of a plant to maintain vigor, shape the plant, or spur new growth.

pruners
Any of several tools used to cut back branches, including pruning shears, loppers, and saws.

prunifolius, -a, -um
As a species name, means "with leaves like cherry leaves," such as those of the black haw viburnum, *Viburnum prunifolium.*

pruning saw
A saw with a relatively long and narrow cutting blade that can get into tight places.

pruning shears
Handheld pruners, used for removing small twigs, stems, and branches.

Prunus

The botanical name for cherry, almond, plum, peach, and apricot.

pseudobulb

The swollen, stemlike, often grooved base of many orchids. It usually stores the water and food on which the plant thrives during the dry season.

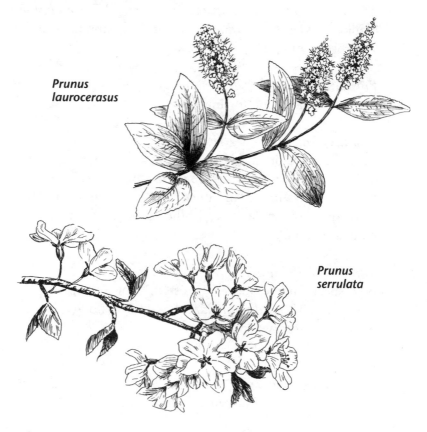

Prunus
laurocerasus

Prunus
serrulata

Pseudotsuga

The botanical name for Douglas fir.

pubescent

Hairy or downy.

puddling
An old method, messy but effective, of protecting fine
feeder roots when transplanting. Its object is to coat all the
roots with a thin film of wet soil, by dipping them into a
soupy mixture of loam and water (mud), just before
planting.

pulch-
As part of a species name, means "pretty." For example,
blanket flower, *Gaillardia pulchella,* is an annual wildflower
with pretty blossoms.

Pulmonaria
The botanical name for lungwort.

pumilus, -a, -um
As a species, cultivar, or variety name, means "small or
dwarf." For example, the Japanese stone pine, *Pinus
pumila,* grows broad and bushy and never gets tall. Dwarf
cultivars of other pines (and other conifers, too) are often
named 'Pumila'.

punctatus, -a, -um
As a species name, means "spotted." For example, spotted
horsemint, *Monarda punctata,* has yellow flowers marked
with purple-brown spots.

pungens
As a species name, means "sharp-pointed." For example,
the Colorado or blue spruce, *Picea pungens,* has very sharp
needles.

Punica
The botanical name for pomegranate.

purpureus, -a, -um

As a species name, means "purple." For example, purple coneflower, *Echinacea purpurea,* has pink-purple ray flowers.

Pyracantha

The botanical name for firethorn.

Pyracantha

pyrethrin

A natural contact insecticide made from the ground-up flowers of the pyrethrum daisies. It is the active ingredient in most ready-to-use household and houseplant insecticides and is moderately toxic to animals.

pyriform

Pear shaped.

Pyrus

The botanical name for pear.

Quercus

quercifolius, -a, -um
As a species name, means "with leaves shaped like oak leaves," as on the oak-leaved scented geranium, *Pelargonium quercifolium*.

Quercus
The botanical name for oak.

quilled
Having a petal shape like that of a quill pen. Cactus-flowered dahlias, for example, have quilled petals.

raceme
A long inflorescence with individual flowers borne on short, unbranched side stalks off a larger central stalk.

raceme

rachis
The central axis of a compound leaf or frond to which the leaflets are attached.

radicans
As a species name, means "with stems that send out roots." Usually applies to woody vines such as trumpet creeper, *Campsis radicans,* that can spread over the ground or climb vertically.

radicle
The primary root of a plant, developed in a seedling; the embryonic root of a seedling.

rain gauge
A device for measuring the amount of rainfall.

raised bed
Any garden bed that is built up higher than the surrounding soil, usually supported by boards, stones, bricks, blocks, or other edging.

ray

Rancho Santa Ana Botanic Garden
The largest botanic garden to focus on plants native to California. This private research and educational institution was founded in 1927 in Claremont, California. A spectacular display of the state's wildflowers is a major attraction from March through May.

Ranunculus
The botanical name for buttercup.

Raulston, J. C. (1940–1996)
Director of the North Carolina State University Arboretum and one of the most influential horticulturists of the late 20th century. His passion was to extend the public's interest beyond the suburban monoculture to incorporate

worthy but uncommon species; to that end he wrote and lectured extensively and also answered thousands of letters and phone calls each year. *See also* **North Carolina State University Arboretum.**

ray
One of the flat marginal florets in an aster, daisy, sunflower, or other composite flower head, as distinguished from the central disk florets. *See also* **disk.**

receptacle
The expanded tip of a flower stalk or axis that bears the floral organs or the group of flowers in a head. Occasionally, as in strawberries, the receptacle develops into a fruitlike form.

recurved
Curved downward or backward. Refers to petals, leaves, or hairs. Also called reflexed.

reed-sedge peat
See **peat moss.**

reflexed
See **recurved.**

regular flower
A flower with petals and sepals arranged around the center like the spokes of a wheel and that is thus radially symmetrical. *See also* **actinomorphic.**

remontant
A plant that flowers more than once a year. Used particularly to distinguish modern reflowering roses from the old-fashioned ones that bloomed only once a year. Also called repeat bloomer.

renewal pruning
A technique for reviving old, overgrown shrubs by cutting them down to the ground in early spring. Some, but not all, shrubs respond to this with a flush of new growth.

repeat bloomer
See remontant.

repellent
A chemical or other product used on or near plants in the hope (often illusory) that it will keep animals from eating the plants. Soap bars, human hair, and lion's urine are a few of the many repellents supposed to keep away deer.

repens or *reptans*
As a species name, means "creeping." For example, both creeping holly grape, *Mahonia repens,* and bugleweed, *Ajuga reptans,* spread by underground runners and make good ground covers.

Mahonia repens

resin
The thick viscous secretion of many conifers that hardens in contact with air.

resistant
A term used to describe a plant bred to, or naturally able to, resist a particular disease such as fusarium or fire blight.

respiration
The chemical process by which animals and plants release the energy that is stored in carbohydrates and other foodstuffs. In respiration, oxygen is taken up and carbon dioxide is given off.

resting period
A period of suspended growth or dormancy, needed by many plants to induce subsequent flowering.

restoration ecology
The process of nurturing degraded ecosystems back to health. *See also* **Leopold, Aldo.**

resupinate
A term used to describe a flower that is twisted or upside down. The vast majority of orchids are resupinate.

retaining wall
Any wall constructed to hold back soil. Such walls are often used to terrace a sloping piece of land.

reticulate
Netlike or weblike. Often refers to leaves that are covered with a prominent network or webbing of veins. Can also refer to a netlike membrane that covers corms or other plant parts.

revert

To change back to normal, as when a plant of a cultivar that has been selected for dwarf growth, variegated foliage, double flowers, or other special features sends up one or more shoots that look like the ordinary species.

Rhamnus

The botanical name for buckthorn.

rhiz-

As part of a Latin name, refers to the roots or rhizomes. For example, bigroot geranium, *Geranium macrorrhizum,* has thick rhizomes.

rhizome

A horizontal underground stem, often swollen into a storage organ. Both roots and shoots emerge from rhizomes. Rhizomes generally branch as they creep along and can be divided to make new plants.

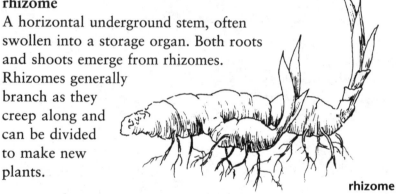

rhizome

Rhododendron

The botanical name for rhododendron and azalea.

Rhus

The botanical name for sumac and poison ivy.

rib

The main vein or any prominent ridge or vein of a leaf or other plant organ.

Rhododendron

Ribes
The botanical name for currant and gooseberry.

riddle
A large-meshed sieve, often round but sometimes square or oblong, used to screen out rocks and twigs from soil or compost.

Rhus

Robinia

The botanical name for locust.

Robinson, William (1838–1935)

An Irishman often credited with revolutionizing the gardens of England. He was a superb plantsman who is remembered today for encouraging the gardeners of his adopted country to forsake the formality of the bedding-out garden, with its blobs of color and formal clipped hedges. His emphasis on informality and subtle color combinations shaped many of the ideas later made popular by his friend Gertrude Jekyll.

robustus, -a, -um

As a species name, means "stout or strong." For example, the Mexican fan palm, *Washingtonia robusta,* has a trunk that looks even thicker than it is because it is surrounded with a layer of fronds that have died and turned brown, but not fallen off.

Washingtonia robustus

rock garden
A landscape created with rocks and alpine plants (small plants native to mountainous regions).

Rodale, J. I. (Jerome Irving) (1898–1971)
An IRS accountant turned industrialist, and an avid advocate of preventive medicine. In 1942 he launched what was then a controversial magazine, *Organic Gardening,* to teach people how to raise healthful food by fostering healthy soil.

rogue
1. A plant that is different from (and usually inferior to) typical members of its species or cultivar.
2. To destroy atypical, or rogue, plants.

root
The underground portion of a plant that serves to anchor it and to absorb water and dissolved nutrients from the soil.

root ball
The roots of a container-grown plant or dug-up plant along with the soil that surrounds them.

root-bound
A term used to describe a plant that has been left too long in a too-small container, so the roots are densely crowded and often tangled or coiled. This stunts growth, but if the roots are loosened and spread out when the plant is transplanted, it usually recovers.

root crops
Plants whose edible portion is the root; for example, parsnips, carrots, and beets.

root cutting
A piece of the root used for propagation. This method of
producing new plants is especially useful for plants that
tend to sucker, such as blackberries and raspberries.

root hairs
The invisible hairs on tip ends of roots through which the
plant absorbs water and dissolved nutrients.

rooting hormone
An auxin or similar natural or synthetic compound that
stimulates cuttings to produce roots and thus greatly
enhances the vegetative propagation of new plants.
Synthetic rooting hormones are available in both powder
and liquid form. Besides hastening the initiation of roots,
they increase the number and quality of those formed.

root pruning
Cutting back the roots of trees either to prepare them for
future transplanting, by forcing the root ball to send out
further feeder roots within a circumscribed area, or in some
cases to stimulate the flowering of barren fruit trees or
ornamentals.

root rot
Any of several fungal diseases liable to infect plants
growing in poorly drained soil.

root run
See root zone.

rootstock
An underground stem with eyes (buds) for next season's
growth and with roots. Also called a rhizome. "Rootstock"
is also a term for the underground base stock on which a

desirable variety is grafted, as in rose and fruit culture. In this case, it is also called an understock.

root zone
The area in the soil occupied by the roots of a plant. Also called root run.

Rosaceae
The rose family, which in addition to roses includes many of our most important fruiting and ornamental plants, among them apples, crab apples, pears, cherries, and raspberries.

rosarian
One who specializes in the cultivation and propagation of roses.

rosary
A Victorian word for a rose garden.

rose
1. A plant of the genus *Rosa*.

1. rose

2. A nozzle attached to a watering can to produce a soft spray of water.

rosette
A low flat cluster of leaves arranged like the petals of a rose. Many biennials, such as foxgloves and mullein, produce rosettes.

roseus, -a, -um
As a species name, means "pink." For example, the Madagascar periwinkle, *Catharanthus roseus,* typically has pink flowers.

Rosmarinus
The botanical name for rosemary.

rotation
See **crop rotation.**

rotenone
A natural contact insecticide made from the roots of a tropical plant. It kills beneficial as well as destructive insects, is moderately toxic to humans and other warm-blooded animals, and is highly toxic to birds and fish.

rosette

rototiller
A machine with rotary tines, used to loosen soil and incorporate amendments, or to uproot weeds.

rotund-
As part of a species name, means "rounded." For example, button fern, *Pellaea rotundifolia,* a popular greenhouse plant or houseplant, has fronds lined with two rows of neat rounded segments.

row cover
A lightweight spun-fabric cloth that allows water and light to reach plants but that warms the soil and keeps out flying insect pests. Row covers are generally used on food crops to permit the grower to get an early start in spring and to extend the season in fall.

Royal Botanic Gardens
See **Kew Gardens**.

Royal Horticultural Society (RHS)
England's most prestigious plant-related organization. It sponsors the famous Chelsea Flower Show and recently published the 3-million-word, four-volume *New RHS Dictionary of Gardening*. Its official garden, Wisley, is in Surrey.

rubr-
As part of a species name, means "red." For example, the red maple, *Acer rubrum,* has red flowers and fruits and red fall foliage. The redleaf rose, *Rosa rubrifolia,* has reddish leaves and stems.

Rudbeckia

Rubus

The botanical name for raspberry, blackberry, and other bramble fruits.

Rudbeckia

The botanical name for coneflower.

rugosus, -a, -um

As a species name, means "wrinkled." Usually refers to leaves, such as the heavily veined, wrinkled-looking foliage of the rugosa rose, *Rosa rugosa*.

runner

A slender shoot that grows along the ground, forming roots and a new plant at its tip end.

running grass

See **sod-forming grass**.

runoff

Water that is applied to the soil too quickly or for too long a time and thus runs off and is wasted; fertilizer or pesticide that is washed from a field, a lawn, or garden soil into rivers or other waterways.

rust
Any of a number of fungal diseases that cause rusty-looking spots on leaves or stems, particularly in cool damp weather.

Ruta
The botanical name for rue.

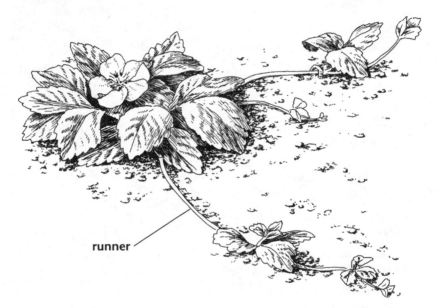

runner

sabadilla
A natural contact insecticide made from the powdered seeds of a Mexican plant. In high doses it is toxic to bees, and sabadilla dust can cause an allergic reaction in humans.

Sabal
The botanical name for palmetto.

Sackville-West, Vita (1892–1962)
English poet and novelist famous in her lifetime for her writings (and her associations with other women) and today—at least among gardeners—celebrated for the gardens she created at Sissinghurst Castle, in Kent, England. With her husband, Harold Nicolson, she transformed a weed-filled Elizabethan ruin into the ultimate English garden. Perhaps her most famous planting is Sissinghurst's White Garden.

salicifolius, -a, -um
As a species name, means "with leaves shaped like willow leaves," such as those of the willowleaf cotoneaster, *Cotoneaster salicifolius*.

Salix
The botanical name for willow.

Sabal

salt marsh hay
Hay made from the grasses that grow in coastal marshes, a valuable mulch since it contains no weed seeds and does not pack down as much as ordinary hay. Also called marsh hay. *See also* **hay; straw.**

Salvia
The botanical name for sage.

Salvia

samara
A dry winged seed, either single, like that of the elm, or double, like that of the maple. Also called key.

Sambucus
The botanical name for elderberry.

sand
The worn grains of rock, the largest of the three minerals that form the basis of soil. The other two are silt and clay.

sandy soil
Soil with large particles that drains quickly but holds nutrients poorly.

sanguin-
As part of a Latin name, means "blood colored." For example, bloodroot, *Sanguinaria canadensis,* has bright red sap in the roots. Blood-twig dogwood, *Cornus sanguinea,* has twigs with dark red bark.

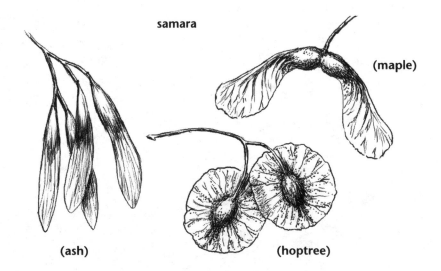

samara

(maple)

(ash)   (hoptree)

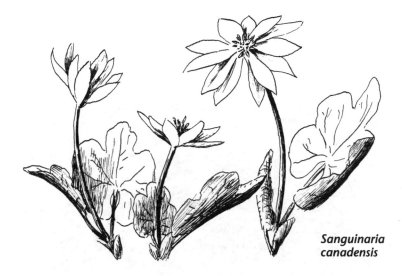

Sanguinaria canadensis

Santolina
The botanical name for lavender cotton.

sap
The fluid in plants.

sapling
A young tree.

Saponaria
The botanical name for soapwort.

saprophyte
A plant, such as a fungus, that feeds on dead or decaying organic matter. Saprophytes have no chlorophyll.

sapwood
In a tree, the layer of usually light-colored wood between the interior heartwood and the bark, through which water and nutrients are carried.

Sasa

Sargent, Charles Sprague (1841–1927)
Founding director of the Arnold Arboretum, with which he
was associated for 54 years and which by the time of his
death had become one of the great plant-study resources in
North America. He was a plant explorer as well as an
authority on native trees (and his advocacy for the
protection of forest land shaped federal policy at the end of
the 19th century). Many plants are named in his honor,
among them the Sargent crab apple, *Malus sargentii;* the
Sargent cherry, *Prunus sargentii;* and the Sargent juniper,
Juniperus sargentii.

Sarracenia
The botanical name for pitcher plant.

Sasa
The botanical name for running bamboo.

sativus, -a, -um
As a species name, means "cultivated." Often refers to food crops or culinary herbs, such as garlic, *Allium sativum.*

Satureja
The botanical name for savory.

sawfly
A wasplike insect whose larvae feed on the foliage and fruit of many trees and shrubs.

saxatilis, -e
As a species name, means "found among rocks." For example, basket-of-gold, *Aurinia saxatilis,* grows well along the top of a rock retaining wall.

scab
Any of several fungal diseases that cause rough raised spots on leaves or fruits. Apple scab is a common problem.

Scabiosa
The botanical name for pincushion flower.

scaffolding
On fruit trees especially, limiting the number of branches that extend from the trunk, so the tree will be able to support the weight of its fruit.

scald
A superficial discoloration on fruits, vegetables, leaves, or tree trunks caused by sudden exposure to intense sunlight, often following pruning or storm damage, or by moving a container-grown plant to a sunnier site.

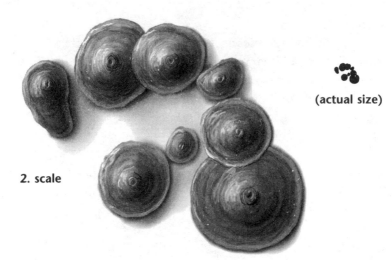

(actual size)

2. scale

scale
1. A small, often dry, leaf or bract.
2. A small inconspicuous sucking insect. There are hundreds of kinds of scale insects. They are serious pests of trees and shrubs, especially in mild climates.

scandent
A term used to describe a plant without tendrils that climbs by intertwining its stems through other plants, such as vining honeysuckle, Carolina jessamine, or wisteria.

scape
A flower stalk that grows directly from the base of a plant, as in daffodils and daylilies. It is usually leafless.

scar
A mark indicating a former attachment, as of a leaf to a stem.

scarecrow
A crude image or effigy of a person — often entertainingly dressed — that is set up in a farm field or garden to scare crows and other birds away from food plants.

scarecrow

scarify
To penetrate hard seed coats by scratching or nicking the seeds or immersing them briefly in hot water, acid, or bleach.

Scilla
The botanical name for squill.

scion
A detached shoot of a woody plant, containing two or more buds, to be used in grafting. As distinguished from a cutting, which will be rooted, a scion is inserted in a stock (a living plant). When scion and stock have been completely united, the buds of the scion will continue to produce growth similar to that of the plant from which it was cut, not that of the stock onto which it was grafted.

sclerosis
The hardening of cells by the formation of a secondary wall and the deposit of lignin; woodiness. Also called sclerification.

scopulorum
As a species name, means "native to rocky sites or cliffsides," as is the Rocky Mountain juniper, *Juniperus scopulorum*.

scorch
A browning between the veins or along the edges of leaves caused by hot weather, spider mite damage, excess or insufficient nutrients, or pesticide damage.

scree
An accumulation of rocky detritus on a hillside or at the base of a slope. In gardening, scree is a mixture of gravel, small stones, and sand for growing alpine plants.

scrub
A growth of scraggly stunted trees and shrubs, usually associated with extreme climatic conditions and very shallow soil.

scurfy
Covered with tiny broad scales. Usually refers to stems or leaves of woody plants.

scythe
A long, curved, single-edged blade with a long bent handle, used for cutting tall grass or reaping grain.

scythe

seaweed
Any of various marine algae or plants. Seaweed makes an excellent high-potash fertilizer.

secateurs
The English term for handheld pruning shears. Usually considered an affectation when used by North Americans.

secondary growth
Growth that results in the thickening of a stem, stalk, or root, produced by cell divisions in the vascular cambium. *See also* **cambium; primary growth.**

secondary nutrients
The macronutrients other than nitrogen (chemical symbol N), phosphorus (P), and potassium (K) needed by plants — namely, calcium (Ca), magnesium (Mg), and sulfur (S). *See also* **primary nutrients; macronutrients; complete fertilizer.**

sedge
A grasslike plant. Most sedges have three-angled stems, giving rise to the phrase "Sedges have edges."

Sedum
The botanical name for stonecrop.

seed
A fertilized ripened ovule, almost always covered with a protective coating and contained in a fruit.

seed bank
An organization dedicated to keeping old varieties of plants alive and available to breeders and gardeners by preserving seeds of these plants.

seed-grown
A term used to describe a plant grown from seed, not by vegetative propagation.

seed leaf
The first leaf or one of a pair of leaves produced by the embryo of a seed plant. In many dicots such as marigolds, the emerging shoot lifts the two cotyledons above ground, where they expand, turn green, and function as the seedling's first leaves. Seed leaves are always opposite, simple, and entire, regardless of how the subsequent, or true, leaves will look. *See also* **first true leaves.**

seedling
An infant plant; a plant raised from seed.

Seed Savers Exchange
Founded in 1975 in Decorah, Iowa, the largest nongovernmental organization in the world working to save heirloom varieties of vegetables and fruits from extinction.

seed viability
See **viability.**

selection
The practice by which growers select seed from only the best plants, continuing the process over the years to produce a superior strain.

selective weed killer
An herbicide that kills some plants but not others. Such herbicides are often used on lawns to kill broad-leaved weeds without damaging the grasses.

seed-grown

self-branching
A term used to describe mostly annuals or perennials that produce numerous side shoots, form bushy rounded plants automatically, and do not require pinching or pruning. These plants lack apical dominance.

selfing
Manually pollinating a flower by placing its pollen on its own stigma. *See also* **self-pollination**.

self-pollination
The transfer of pollen from one flower to the same or other flowers on the same plant. *See also* **cross-pollination**.

self-seed
To produce seeds that germinate and grow with no care from the gardener.

semievergreen
Retaining at least some green foliage well into winter; shedding leaves in a cold climate but not where winters are mild.

semihardwood cutting
A cutting taken from the new growth of a woody plant after the stems have partially matured and are stiff, not soft. Depending on latitude, these cuttings are usually taken between mid-July and early September.

sempervirens
As a species name, means "evergreen." For example, the perennial candytuft, *Iberis sempervirens,* has foliage that stays bright green all year.

senescence
The aging of a plant after it reaches maturity, leading eventually to its death. Usually refers to annuals after they set seed.

sensitive
A term used to describe a plant or plant part that responds to touch. The carnivorous plants that trap insects that land on them are an (extreme) example. The sensitive plant, *Mimosa pudica,* is another.

sepal
One of the outermost series of flower parts, arranged in a ring outside the petals. It is often small, green, and leaflike but is sometimes large and colorful. Collectively, the sepals make up the calyx.

Sequoiadendron
The botanical name for giant sequoia.

serrate
Having sharp, forward-pointing teeth on the margin. Usually refers to leaves.

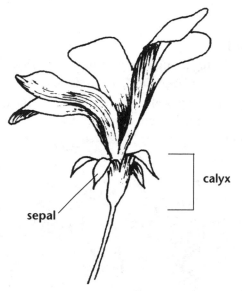

calyx

sepal

sessile
Stalkless; attached directly to the main stem.

set
A small onion or shallot bulb planted instead of seeds for a quicker crop.

shade
See **dappled shade; full shade; half shade; high shade; light shade.**

shade tree
A tree planted for the shade it casts, as opposed to one selected for its ornamental flowers or its fruits. Some of the most popular shade trees are maples, oaks, and lindens.

Shakespeare garden
A garden featuring the flowers in Shakespeare's plays and sonnets, which are full of references to flowers and scenes set in gardens.

sharp sand

A sand with sharp angular grains, not smooth round ones. It is used for starting seeds or cuttings or for improving the drainage of potting soils. Also called builder's sand, as distinguished from beach sand, which has no use in horticulture.

Shortia

sheaf

A bundle of grasses or cereal plants.

shear

To prune with long-bladed shears, cutting back all the stems, sometimes severely, to a uniform level or plane.

sheath

Any tubular or sheathing organ, often leaflike or membranous, that surrounds the base of a stalk or helps to form one. Sheaths are common in the grasses and palms but infrequent among dicots.

shelter belt

See **windbreak**.

shoot
An aboveground stem, either the main stem or a side one.

short-day plant
A plant that flowers when the days grow short, such as chrysanthemums or Japanese anemones. *See also* **photoperiodism.**

Shortia
The botanical name for Oconee bells.

short-lived perennial
A plant that tends to live only a few years, although it often persists by self-seeding. Columbines and violas are examples of short-lived perennials.

shovel
A tool with a long handle and a broad scoop or blade, used for digging and for moving dirt.

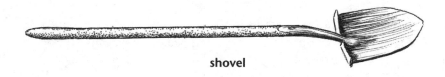

shovel

shredder
A machine that chops up soft stems and leaves so that they can be used as mulch or added to the compost pile. *See also* **chipper.**

shrub
A woody plant that is shorter than a tree and usually has several stems that branch from the base. These are not hard-and-fast distinctions; a tree may have two or more

trunks. For example, the cornelian cherry, *Cornus mas,* is generally described as a shrub although it easily grows to 25 feet. The Sargent crab apple, *Malus sargentii,* may top out at 12 feet but is generally considered a tree. In these cases, a plant is often described as a shrub or small tree, depending on how it is used in the landscape and whether or not the lower branches have been removed. *See also* **bush.**

shrubbery
Usually, a row or border of shrubs, allowed to grow naturally.

sibling
An orchid that is related to another orchid by virtue of having been produced from the same seedpod.

sickle
A short-handled cutting tool with a sharp, hook-shaped blade, used primarily to cut grasses or grain crops.

side-dress
To apply granular fertilizer to the soil alongside a plant or row of plants during the growing season to stimulate them.

Siebold, Philipp Franz von (1796–1866)
German doctor who traveled extensively in Japan and introduced many Japanese plants to Western gardens, such as the lovely Oyama magnolia, *Magnolia sieboldii.*

Silphium
The botanical name for compass plant and prairie dock.

silt
Soil with medium-size mineral particles, larger than clay and smaller than sand.

simple leaf

simple leaf
A leaf with only one blade. It may be toothed, scalloped, or lobed but is never divided all the way to the leafstalk. *See also* **compound leaf.**

sinensis, -e
As a species name, means "native to China." For example, China tea, *Camellia sinensis,* is native to China but is now grown on plantations in mild climates around the world.

Sissinghurst
The home and garden of Vita Sackville-West, today one of England's most famous garden tourist attractions. It is notable for, among other things, its White Garden.

Sisyrinchium
The botanical name for blue-eyed grass.

six-pack
See **cell pack.**

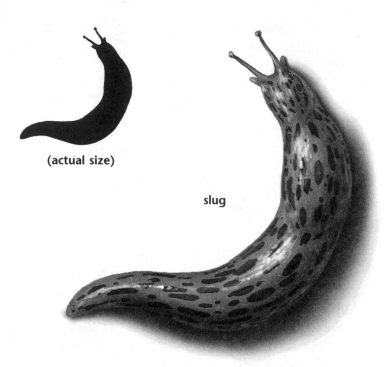

(actual size)

slug

skep
A straw or wicker beehive, these days most often used as an ornament in an herb garden.

sleep movements
The folding together of leaves, leaflets, or petals at night or on cloudy days. For example, crocuses, gazanias, moss rose, and many other flowers close at night and reopen the following day. Mimosa trees, clover, garden beans, and many other plants have leaves that fold up or down at night.

slip
A cutting taken for grafting or rooting.

slow-release fertilizer
A natural fertilizer that releases nutrients gradually, over a period of time. Bonemeal is an example, but blood meal, by contrast, gives fast results. *See also* **controlled-release fertilizer.**

sludge
An organic fertilizer made from dried processed sewage.

slug
A slimy, night-feeding mollusk without a shell that feeds on plants. It thrives in shady moist soil.

Smilacina
The botanical name for false Solomon's seal.

snail
A gastropod closely related to the slug, but with a shell. It feeds on plants at night.

Smilacina

soaker hose
A rubber or plastic hose with perforations to let water seep into the ground; a porous canvas hose.

sod
A section of grass-covered surface soil held together by matted roots; turf.

sod-forming grass
A lawn grass that spreads by sending out stolons (horizontal stems that creep above ground) or rhizomes (underground stems). Also called running grass.

sod webworm

(actual size)

sod webworm
A larva that feeds on leaves of grass.

softwood
The wood produced by coniferous trees and shrubs such as pines or Douglas fir, used mostly for construction or lumber, not as firewood. *See also* **hardwood; conifer**.

softwood cutting
A cutting taken from young, soft, but not too succulent tips or stems of herbaceous or woody plants. This is the most frequently used type of cutting, because it roots very readily.

soil
The thin layer of weathered rock particles and organic matter, containing water and tiny air spaces, that covers the earth and provides support and nutrients for plants.

soil amendment
Any bulk material incorporated into the soil. Such materials are usually intended to improve structure, drainage, or aeration, but they may also contain nutrients.

soil horizon
The layers in the upper crust of the earth. The differences in the horizons are most easily seen in soils that have not been touched in decades. The top, or O, horizon is the layer of undecomposed litter; the A horizon is topsoil, where most roots grow; B is the subsoil; and C is the parent rock material, broken into chunks. Although some roots can penetrate into the C horizon, few microorganisms live there.

soilless gardening
Growing plants with their roots immersed in containers of a nutrient solution rather than soil. Also called hydroponics.

soilless mix
A medium for growing plants in containers. It contains no actual soil but includes various combinations of ingredients such as peat moss, composted pine bark, sand, perlite, or

vermiculite, plus small amounts of limestone and other ground minerals or fertilizers. Nurseries and professional horticulturists prefer soilless mixes because they weigh less than garden soil, provide much better drainage in containers, are consistent from batch to batch, and are not contaminated with weed seeds or disease organisms. *See also* **Cornell mix.**

soil profile
The layers, or horizons, of the soil at any given point. *See also* **soil horizon.**

soil sample
Several trowelfuls of soil, mixed together, to represent the soil typical throughout a garden, plot, or field.

Solidago

soil test
A method of measuring the pH of and the nutrients in the soil.

soil-test kit
A kit that may be purchased for home testing of soil samples.

solarization
A nontoxic method of killing weeds and insect pests by covering the ground with layers of clear plastic and allowing the sun to create enough heat to destroy all of the living organisms — good and bad — in the soil.

Solidago
The botanical name for goldenrod.

solitary
Borne singly or alone, not in clusters.

soluble fertilizer
A powdered synthetic fertilizer that is mixed with water and poured on the soil or sprayed on the foliage. Such solutions are commonly used for houseplants and other plants growing in containers, but they can also be used throughout the garden. Manure tea and other liquid forms of organic fertilizers are used similarly.

sooty mildew
A type of fungus that forms dusty, dark gray spots or scum on the surface of leaves and stems. It is especially common on plants that are infested with aphids or other sucking insects that excrete honeydew, as the mildew consumes the sugars in the honeydew.

Sophora

Sophora
The botanical name for the pagoda or scholar tree.

Sorbus
The botanical name for mountain ash.

sour soil
An old-fashioned term used to describe exceedingly acid, unhealthy soil, which sometimes has a sour smell. *See also* **sweet soil.**

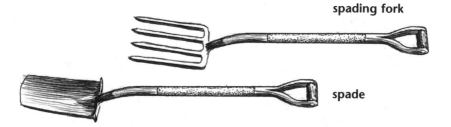

spading fork

spade

spade
A sturdy digging tool with a thick handle and a heavy flat blade that can be pressed into the ground with the foot.

spading fork
A broad-tined fork, useful for digging into sod, for harvesting potatoes or root crops, or for mixing amendments into the soil.

spadix
A fleshy clublike spike bearing minute flowers, usually enclosed within a sheathlike spathe, characteristic of aroid plants such as calla and jack-in-the-pulpit.

spathe
A leaflike bract that encloses a flower cluster or spadix, as, for example, on the peace lily, *Spathiphyllum*.

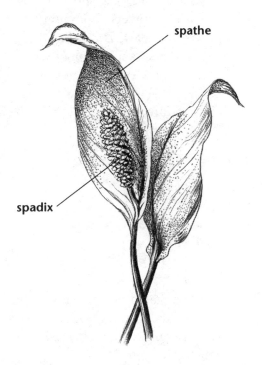

species
A group of individual plants that share many characteristics and interbreed freely. The species is the basic unit in plant classification. An individual plant is described by two Latin words; the first indicates the genus, the second the species. *See also* **Linnaeus, Carolus; genus.**

species name
See specific epithet.

specific epithet
The second word in the Latin binomial name for a plant, designating the species. Often called species name.

specimen plant
A plant placed conspicuously alone, usually in a prominent place, to show off its ornamental qualities.

speciosus, -a, -um or ***spectabilis, -e***
As a species name, means "showy." For example, the southern catalpa tree, *Catalpa speciosa,* has very showy clusters of white flowers. Common bleeding heart, *Dicentra spectabilis,* is a perennial with showy pink or white flowers.

spike

sphagnum moss
See peat moss.

sphagnum peat
See peat moss.

spider mite
See mite.

spike
An elongated flower cluster with individual flowers borne on very short stalks or attached directly to the main stem.

spine
A strong, sharp, stiff projection, usually from the stem or leaf of a plant but sometimes from the calyx or fruit. Thistles, hollies, and cacti have spines.

Spiranthes
The botanical name for ladies' tresses.

spit
A spadeful of soil; the depth of soil equal to the length of a spade's blade.

spoiled hay
See **hay**.

spore
The microscopic body by which ferns, mosses, lichens, fungi, and algae reproduce. Spores are smaller than even the tiniest seeds.

sport
A plant or sometimes just a branch or shoot of a plant that shows a marked change from the normal, typically as a result of mutation. Sports are often the source of new cultivars. *See also* **mutant**.

spp.
The plural abbreviation for "species."

spreader
A device used to spread fertilizer or seeds, usually over a lawn.

spreading plant
A plant whose branches grow in a more or less horizontal direction.

sprig
An ornamental small branch, usually but not always including flowers or berries.

sprout
1. The first shoot from a seed.
2. To begin to grow; to send out a new shoot from a seed or bud.

spruce budworm
A caterpillar that is a serious pest on several conifers, including firs, hemlocks, and pines, in addition to spruces.

spruce
budworm

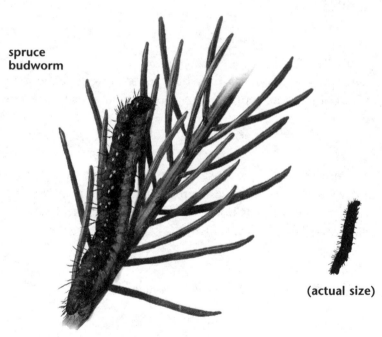

(actual size)

spur
1. A tubular elongation of the petals or sepals of certain flowers, usually containing nectar. Columbine is an example of a flower with spurs.
2. A short, specialized fruit-bearing branchlet present on apple trees and some other kinds of trees.

squamous
Scaly; covered with scales.

square-foot gardening
A popular system for arranging the plants in a vegetable garden that simplifies planning and makes very efficient use of space.

Stachys
The botanical name for lamb's ears.

stalk
Loosely, the stem of any organ. When used accurately, the term "stalk" has several specialized meanings: a leafstalk is properly a petiole; a flower stalk may be a peduncle, a pedicel, or a scape; the stalk of an anther is properly called a filament; the stalk of a fern frond is usually called a stipe.

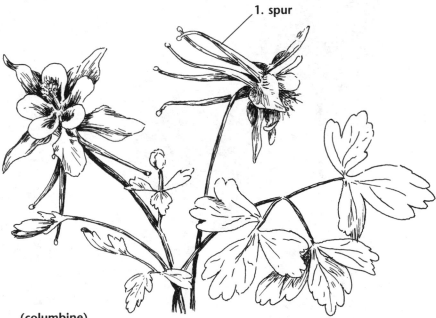

1. spur

(columbine)

stamen

The male reproductive organ of a flower, including the anther, where pollen is produced, and the filament, which supports the anther.

staminate

Male, having stamens. Can refer to male plants, which bear only male flowers, or to the flowers themselves.

standard

1. A plant trained to grow a round bushy head of branches atop a single upright stem.
2. A full-size fruit tree.
3. The erect central petals of irises and related flowers.

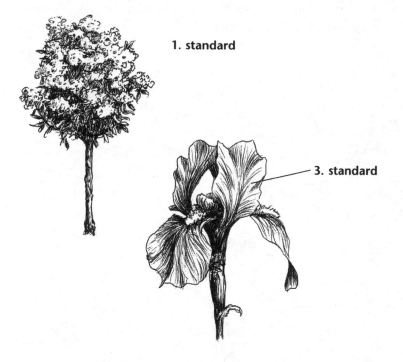

1. standard

3. standard

stem
The main axis of a plant from which leaves and flowers grow. Stems can take many forms, from the trunk of a pine tree to the runners of a honeysuckle vine or the creeping rhizome of an iris.

stem cutting
A cutting that includes one or more nodes and internodes, taken from the stem of a plant but not including its apex or tip, used for propagation.

sterile
1. A term used to describe a flower without functional sexual parts.
2. A term used to describe a plant that is unable to produce seeds, often because it is of hybrid ancestry.
3. A term used to describe soil that has been heated to a temperature high enough to destroy weed seeds or pathogens.
4. A term used to describe a growing medium that is not contaminated by pathogens.

stigma
The receptive apex of the pistil of a flower, on which pollen is deposited.

stinkbug
Any of several triangular-shaped bugs that suck plant juices from leaves, stems, buds, or fruit and release a strong unpleasant odor when crushed or disturbed.

stipe
The stalk of a fern frond.

Stokesia

stipule
One of the usually small, paired appendages at the base of a leafstalk in certain plants, such as roses and beans.

stock
1. A plant or stem onto which a graft is made.
2. A plant from which cuttings are taken or seeds are collected. Nurseries often maintain special stock plants for propagation.

Stokesia
The botanical name for Stoke's aster.

stolon
A stem that runs along the ground, forming roots and new plants at intervals along its length.

stolonifera
As a species name, means "spreading by stolons," as do the shrubby red osier dogwood, *Cornus stolonifera,* and the dainty little strawberry geranium, *Saxifraga stolonifera.*

stoma (plural: **stomata**)
A microscopic pore, located mainly on the undersides of leaves, through which a plant takes in and releases oxygen, carbon dioxide, water vapor, and other gases.

stomach poison
An insecticide that must be ingested in order to work and does not kill insects that simply touch it. Bt is an example.

stone
A single seed surrounded by a large hard shell and covered by pulp. A peach is an example of a stone fruit.

stone sink
See **trough.**

strain
A cultivar that is normally propagated by seed, retaining its desirable traits from one generation to the next.

stratify
To keep seeds under cool, dark, moist conditions for a period of weeks or months so that they will subsequently germinate.

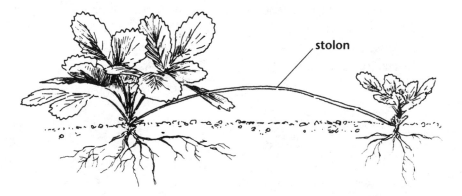

stolon

straw
The dried stems and leaves of cereal grains such as oats, wheat, or rye. It is often used as a mulch in vegetable gardens or to cover grass seed in a newly sown lawn. Straw contains few if any weed seeds and is therefore more desirable than hay. It decomposes quickly and adds organic matter to the soil. *See also* **hay; salt marsh hay.**

strawberry pot
A tall rounded clay pot with holes along the sides into which strawberry plants are rooted. Such pots are often used to grow other plants in a decorative way.

Strelitzia
The botanical name for bird-of-paradise.

strictus, -a, -um
As a species, cultivar, or variety name, means "narrowly erect or upright." For example, porcupine grass, *Miscanthus sinensis* 'Strictus', forms erect clumps of green-and-yellow-striped leaves.

strike
To send out roots. Refers to cuttings.

Strybing Arboretum
A 70-acre botanic garden in San Francisco's Golden Gate Park, with extensive plantings of ornamental trees and shrubs, including California natives and exotics, and many flower beds and greenhouses.

style
The elongated part of a pistil between the stigma and the ovary.

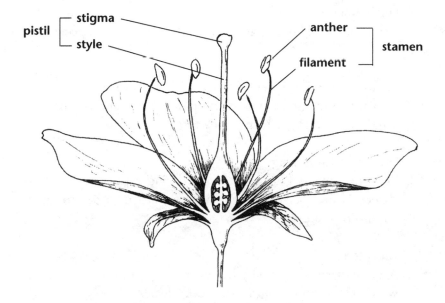

Styrax
The botanical name for snowbell.

suaveolens
As a species name, means "sweet-scented." For example, pineapple mint, *Mentha suaveolens,* has a sweet, fruity aroma.

subshrub
A perennial plant with woody stems at the base and tender new growth that dies back more or less each winter. The term is sometimes wrongly used to describe a low-growing shrub.

subsoil
The mineral soil of decomposed rocks, without any humus, that lies beneath the topsoil.

subspecies
A naturally occurring geographical variant of a species.

substrate
1. An underlying layer. Usually refers to subsoil.
2. A medium used for growing plants, particularly in laboratory experiments.

succession planting
Planting repeated crops of fast-growing vegetables, such as lettuce, a number of days or weeks apart in order to have a continuous supply.

succulent
A plant with thick fleshy leaves or stems that can store water. Cacti and sedums are examples.

sucker
A shoot arising from an underground bud on the roots or rootstock of a plant. Suckers can be removed and replanted

succulent
(*Sedum* x **'Autumn Joy'**)

as new plants. If the sucker grew from the rootstock of a grafted plant, however, the resulting new plant will have the attributes of the original stock, not the desirable graft.

suckering
The tendency of a plant to grow suckers. It is not usually considered a desirable trait.

sunken garden
The lowest and usually central part of a garden built on different levels.

superphosphate
A high-phosphate fertilizer often used when planting because phosphorus is the nutrient most responsible for root growth.

surfactant
A soaplike compound added to water or some other liquid to increase its wetting properties by reducing the surface tension of the droplets. Also called wetting agent.

Sussex trug
See **trug**.

sustainable agriculture
A system of farming or gardening that can be sustained indefinitely without damaging the soil and that does not rely on expensive inputs such as purchased fertilizers, fuel for tractors, or irrigation water. Traditional farmers around the world provide many successful examples. *See also* **permaculture**.

swamp
A seasonally flooded bottomland with more woody plants than a marsh and better drainage than a bog.

sympodial

sweet soil
An old-fashioned term used to denote soil that is limy or alkaline. *See also* **sour soil.**

sylv-
As part of a species name, means "native to woodlands" (although most plants so named need at least part sun and do not thrive in full shade). For example, the European beech, *Fagus sylvatica,* is a major forest tree in Europe. Woodland tobacco, *Nicotiana sylvestris,* is an annual with tall stalks of white flowers that smell wonderful at night.

symbiosis
A relationship between two different organisms, to the benefit of each.

sympodial
One of the two forms of orchid growth (the other is monopodial), wherein new growth branches off the rhizome of a previous growth, and each new growth is capable of bearing an inflorescence. *See also* **monopodial.**

Syringa
The botanical name for lilac.

systemic insecticide
An insecticide that is absorbed into the tissues of a plant and repels or kills most or some kinds of the insects that feed upon it. One treatment is usually effective for weeks or months. *See also* **contact insecticide.**

Syringa

Tagetes
The botanical name for marigold.

tamping
Gently pressing down the soil around the roots of a plant in order to firm it in place.

tankage
Slaughterhouse wastes used for fertilizers.

tannin
A substance in the leaves and bark of some plants that protects against insects and fungi.

tapestry hedge
A hedge made up of massed shrubs with variously colored foliage.

taproot
A long tapering root that has little or no side growth. Taproots are typical of some seedlings, but few mature plants have them.

Taxodium
The botanical name for bald cypress.

Taxodium

taxonomy
The classification of organisms in an ordered system that indicates natural relationships.

Taxus
The botanical name for yew.

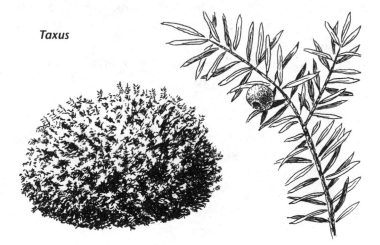

Taxus

Taylor, Norman (1883–1967)
A distinguished botanist and author, long associated with
the New York Botanical Garden and the Brooklyn Botanic
Garden. His major work, first published in 1936, was *The
Garden Dictionary,* later known as *Taylor's Encyclopedia
of Gardening.*

tectorus, -a, -um
As a species name, means "traditionally planted on the
roofs of houses," often as a good-luck charm. The house
leek or hen-and-chicks, *Sempervivum tectorum,* and
Japanese roof iris, *Iris tectorum,* are popular examples that
also grow well at ground level.

tender
Damaged by freezing temperatures.

tender perennial
A perennial plant that is not hardy in cold climates, where
it may be grown as an annual.

tendril
A thin twisting extension by which a plant grasps an object
and clings for support; a modified stem, stipule, or leaf.

tentacle
On carnivorous plants, a sensitive hair or filament that
detects the arrival of an insect.

tent caterpillar
A hairy dark caterpillar that forms weblike tents or bags in
the crotches of tree branches and eats the leaves.

tenui-
As part of a species name, means "slender or thin." For example, moss verbena, *Verbena tenuisecta,* has leaves divided into slender segments.

tepals
Sepals and petals that are similar in size, shape, and color, as in the flowers of tulips, alliums, and many lilies.

terminal
Borne at the tip of a stem or shoot.

terra cotta
From the Italian for "baked earth," a clay flowerpot that has been fired to a reddish brown color but is unglazed, so water and air can penetrate through it.

tent caterpillar

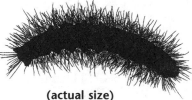

(actual size)

terrarium
A transparent container, tightly fitted with a glass cover, in which plants are grown in soil. Also called bottle garden. *See also* **Wardian case.**

terrestrial
A term used to describe a plant that grows in the ground. Usually used to distinguish orchids and bromeliads with this growth habit from those that are epiphytes, or air plants.

tetraploid
A plant with twice the normal number of chromosomes. Tetraploids are characteristically larger and more vigorous than normal plants.

Teucrium
The botanical name for germander.

Thalictrum
The botanical name for meadow rue.

thatch
Although mistakenly assumed to be caused by grass clippings, actually an impenetrable mat made up of the tough parts of grass plants—the roots, stolons, and rhizomes—that fail to decompose normally. Thick thatch prevents water from reaching the grass roots and harbors insects and disease.

Thaxter, Celia (1835–1894)
A 19th-century New England author and poet. Her fame today rests on just one book, *An Island Garden,* the account of the garden she created on Appledore, one of the Isles of Shoals, located 10 miles off the coast of New

Hampshire. The garden has been restored and is open to the public.

Theophrastus (c. 370–c. 287 B.C.)
Greek philosopher known as the father of botany, and a favorite pupil of Aristotle. He is thought to have written more than 200 books, of which only two survive, *History of Plants* and *Causes of Plants,* and these only in part. But the remarkable thing about them and their author, who also developed the first known botanical garden, is that, almost alone, they carried Greek learning about plants and gardens for 16 centuries, to the Renaissance. Many of his observations are current down to our own time.

thicket
A dense area of scrubby undergrowth and small shrubs and trees.

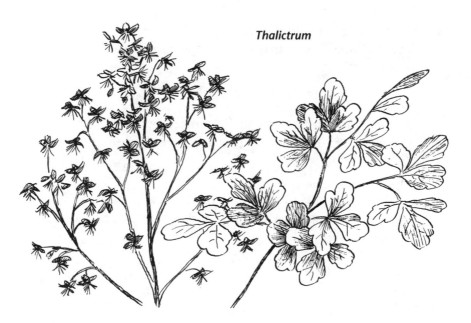

Thalictrum

thimble pot
The British term for the smallest-size clay flowerpot, usually 2 inches by 2 inches.

thinning
Pulling out or cutting off some seedlings in a row, plot, or flat, for the benefit of those that remain.

thinning cut
In pruning, a cut made at the base of a branch or stem to remove it entirely and thus thin the plant.

thin soil
A poor shallow soil deficient in humus or nutrients, or both.

thorn
A sharp woody outgrowth of a stem. Thorns are bigger and tougher than spines or prickles.

thrips (singular and plural)
A tiny slender insect that feeds on leaves, flowers, buds, and stems.

throat
On flowers with partially or fully fused petals, the place where the corolla lobes lead into the corolla tube.

thug
A usually attractive invasive plant that overwhelms more fragile specimens in its vicinity. In the right place and under the right conditions, thugs can be desirable garden perennials.

Thuja
The botanical name for arborvitae.

Tiarella

thumb pot
The British term for a clay pot slightly larger than a thimble pot, measuring about $2\frac{1}{2}$ inches by $2\frac{1}{2}$ inches.

Thunberg, Carl Peter (1743–1829)
Swedish botanist who studied with Linnaeus and then traveled to South Africa and Japan, where he collected many plants that are now in cultivation, such as bush clover, *Lespedeza thunbergii.*

Thymus
The botanical name for thyme.

Tiarella
The botanical name for foamflower.

Tilia
The botanical name for linden.

till
To prepare land for growing plants or crops; to cultivate.

tilth
A fine crumbly soil texture produced by tilling or cultivating. *See also* **friable.**

timed-release fertilizer
See **controlled-release fertilizer.**

timed-release insecticide
An insecticide that is encapsulated in tiny particles that break down gradually, releasing the product over a period of weeks or months.

tinctorius, -a, -um
As a species name, means "used for dyeing yarn or cloth." For example, the annual coreopsis, *Coreopsis tinctoria,* produces bright yellow, orange, and red-brown dyes.

tip cutting
A softwood or semihardwood cutting made from the tip of a shoot, including the apical bud.

tired soil
Soil exhausted of nourishment for a particular crop. The term usually implies that the crop has been grown for too many seasons in one place.

tissue culture
A laboratory technique of propagating new plants from tiny portions of the parent plant.

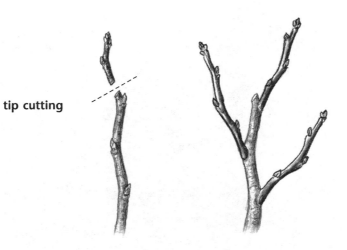

tip cutting

Tithonia
The botanical name for Mexican sunflower.

tomentosus, -a, -um
As a species name, means "densely covered with woolly hairs." For example, the peppermint-scented geranium, *Pelargonium tomentosum,* has leaves that feel like velvet.

toothed
A term used to describe a leaf whose margin is shallowly divided into small toothlike segments. *See also* **lobed; dissected.**

top-dress
1. To apply fertilizer, compost, or manure to the surface of the soil, without turning it under, usually when plants are already growing.
2. To spread fresh soil over a newly seeded patch of lawn.
3. To add fresh potting soil to a container plant, after first removing the top layer of existing soil but without removing the plant from the pot.

topiary

topiary
The art of shearing trees and shrubs into unusual shapes or of training ivy and other creeping plants on shaped wire frames.

topping
In pruning, cutting off most of the crown of a tree without regard to the natural shape. A drastic and unattractive method of pruning, it is often used on too-large trees under power lines.

topsoil
Soil that contains humus as well as mineral elements, as opposed to subsoil, which contains only the latter. *See also* **soil.**

Tower Hill Botanic Garden
Founded in 1986 by the Worcester County Horticultural Society, a 132-acre Massachusetts site featuring an orchard with 119 varieties of heirloom apple trees.

trace elements
See **micronutrients**.

Tradescantia
The botanical name for spiderwort.

trailing
A term used to describe a plant that has long stems that hang down or sweep along the ground, often rooting as they go.

transpiration
The normal escape of water vapor from a plant's leaves, mostly through the stomata (pores). It directly affects growth and wilting, and the plant regulates the rate of transpiration according to its water requirements and the weather.

transplant
1. A seedling or other plant that has reached the stage where it is ready to be transplanted to its permanent site.
2. To move a plant from one place to another or from a container into the ground.

transplant

Tropaeolum

tree
A perennial woody plant with a main trunk and usually a distinct crown. *See also* **shrub**.

tree wrap
A strip of light-colored, porous plastic wrapped around the trunk of a young tree to protect it from sunburn, sudden temperature changes, and gnawing rodents.

treillage
The French name for a lattice or trellis structure used to support vines.

trellis
A form of ornamental slat fence used primarily as a screen or a support for vines. Trellises are one of the earliest forms of garden fence.

trichogramma wasp
A tiny wasp of the genus *Trichogramma,* which lays its eggs inside other insects, including several that are garden pests. As the wasp larvae grow, the pest insect dies.

trickle irrigation
See **drip irrigation.**

trifoliate
With leaflets in groups of three, like clover.

Tropaeolum
The botanical name for nasturtium.

tropical plant
A plant native to the tropics, sometimes grown as a
houseplant in colder climates.

tropism
A reaction to an external stimulus, such as light. *See also*
phototropism; geotropism.

trough
A term that usually refers to the stone cattle or horse
troughs used, primarily by the English, to grow alpine
plants. These, along with stone sinks, became so popular
that authentic ones are virtually unobtainable, but they can
be simulated by concrete or lightweight hypertufa
substitutes.

tropical plant
(Fatsia japonica)

trowel
A hand tool for planting
seedlings or bulbs or for
transplanting small
plants.

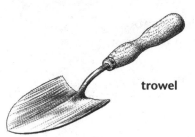

trowel

trug
A shallow oblong English garden basket used to carry fruits
and vegetables. The original Sussex trug was (and still is)
made with willow boards, copper nails, and unpeeled
chestnut rims.

trunk
The stem or axis of a tree.

Tsuga
The botanical name for hemlock.

tuber
A swollen underground storage organ, modified from a
root or rhizome, with buds where new shoots and roots
develop after a dormant period. Examples are potatoes,
dahlias, and tuberous begonias. Also called tuberous root.

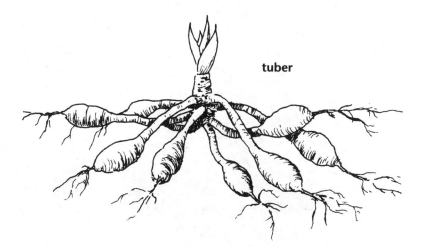

tuber

tubercle
A small tuber; a pealike nodule on the roots of most legumes; a rounded knoblike outgrowth on the ridge or face of many cacti.

tuberosus, -a, -um
As a species name, means "producing tubers." For example, butterfly weed, *Asclepias tuberosa,* develops a very thick tuberous root.

tuberous root
See **tuber.**

tufted
Growing in more or less dense tufts or clusters. No single-stemmed plant can be tufted, but many plants with several stems, such as some grasses, saxifrages, and sedums, are always tufted. When the congestion of stems becomes such as to make the plant into a tight, ball-like cushion, the plant is referred to as a cushion plant.

Tulipa
The botanical name for tulip.

Tulipmania
A craze that occurred in the 1630s in Holland when bulb growers discovered that certain tulip bulbs developed flowers of exceptional beauty—striped, feathered, and wildly colored. Speculation in tulip bulbs among the wealthy Dutch became a national obsession. As the passion for rare tulips raged, the market became so flooded with overpriced bulbs that it collapsed. With so many citizens facing ruin, the government outlawed tulip speculation. Today we know that the unusual flowers were produced by a virus, which can be introduced and controlled.

tunic
A loose membranous outer covering of a bulb or corm, as of the tulip, onion, or crocus.

turf
An area planted with spreading grasses. *See also* **lawn**.

turfgrass
A spreading or stoloniferous grass, as opposed to a tufted ornamental grass. A turfgrass endures, and typically requires, regular mowing.

tussock
A small grass-covered mound.

tuteur
From the French for "trainer," a classic French design for a trellis in the shape of an obelisk.

twig
A small branch.

twining vine
A vine that climbs by wrapping its stem around a support. Twining vines can actually damage or strangle trees.

Ulmus
The botanical name for elm.

Ulmus

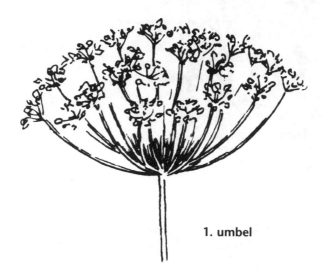

1. umbel

umbel
1. A flower cluster in which the individual flower stalks emerge from the same point on the stem, like the ribs of an umbrella.
2. A member of the family Umbelliferae (formerly called Apiaceae), or carrot family. Carrots, parsley, and dill are examples.

underbrush
See undergrowth.

undergrowth
Low-growing plants, shrubs, and saplings in a forest or woodland. Also called underbrush.

understock
See rootstock.

understory
The smaller, lower trees that grow beneath the major specimens in a woodland or forest.

union
See **graft union.**

unisexual flower
A flower bearing only stamens or pistils, but not both. *See also* **perfect flower.**

United States National Arboretum
A government arboretum situated on 444 acres along the Anacostia River in Washington, D.C. It contains many noteworthy single-genus collections, including 700 species and cultivars of hollies, 500 kinds of crab apples, and 70,000 azalea plants. The 2-acre National Herb Garden features a knot garden and a historic rose garden.

University of California Botanical Garden at Berkeley
An institution founded in 1890 by the university's Botany Department. Its outstanding collections include cacti and succulents, orchids, rhododendrons, and California native plants.

University of Minnesota Landscape Arboretum
An institution located just west of Minneapolis on a 550-acre site. It features display gardens and major collections of crab apples, hostas, ornamental grasses, and many other landscape plants that are hardy to USDA Zone 4.

University of Wisconsin Arboretum
Located in Madison, a leader in the field of restoration ecology, containing the world's oldest restored tall-grass prairie. Its 1,270-acre site is connected by 20 miles of trails and fire lanes and also includes a deciduous oak forest, a conifer forest, and wetlands as well as more-traditional arboretum collections.

USDA

The United States Department of Agriculture.

USDA Hardiness Zone Map

A map issued by the U.S. Department of Agriculture
showing the minimum temperature ranges in the United
States and Canada. *See also* **hardiness zones.**

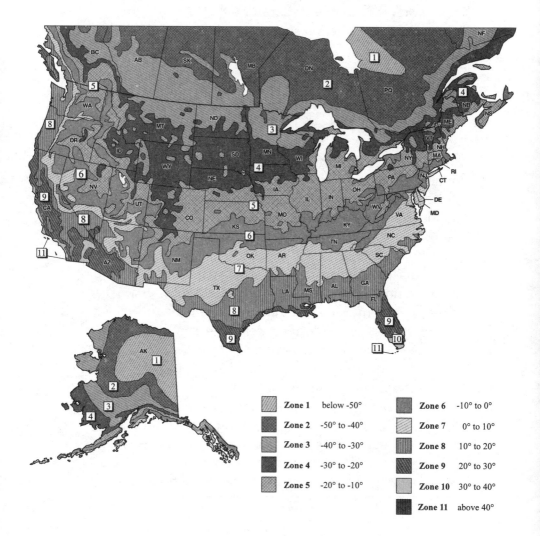

Zone 1	below -50°		**Zone 6**	-10° to 0°
Zone 2	-50° to -40°		**Zone 7**	0° to 10°
Zone 3	-40° to -30°		**Zone 8**	10° to 20°
Zone 4	-30° to -20°		**Zone 9**	20° to 30°
Zone 5	-20° to -10°		**Zone 10**	30° to 40°
			Zone 11	above 40°

Vaccinium
The botanical name for blueberry and cranberry.

variegated
A term used to describe leaves that are marked, striped, or blotched with some color (usually white or yellow) other than green.

Vaccinium

variety

A population of plants that differ consistently from the typical form of the species, occurring naturally in a geographical area. The term is also applied, incorrectly but popularly, to forms produced in cultivation, which are properly called cultivars. A variety is indicated by a third Latin word (sometimes set off by the roman abbreviation "var.") following the two-word term that indicates the genus and species. For example, *Cotoneaster adpressus* var. *praecox* is a more vigorous form of creeping cotoneaster than the normal one. Many plants that used to be considered varieties have been treated as garden plants for so long that they are now considered to be cultivars, and their names are rewritten accordingly.

vascular bundle

A strand of tissue containing both the xylem and the phloem in the young stems, leaves, or flowers of a plant. *See also* **vascular plant**.

vascular plant

Any plant containing food-conducting tissues (the phloem) and water-conducting tissues (the xylem). These include ferns and seed-bearing plants but not mosses or algae.

Vaux-le-Vicomte, Château of

The 17th-century home of Nicolas Fouquet, superintendent of finance during the minority of Louis XIV.

vegetation

Any or all of the plants of an area or a region.

vegetative bud

A bud that contains a leaf or a shoot but not a flower.

**vegetative
propagation**

vegetative propagation
The production of new plants by means other than seeds—
for instance, by rooting stem or leaf cuttings, or by layering
a stem or dividing roots.

vein
One of the vascular bundles or ribs that form the
branching framework of conducting and supporting tissues
in a leaf, flower, or fruit.

velamen
The water-absorbing tissue on the outside of an epiphyte's
roots.

velutinus, -a, -um
As a species name, means "velvety." For example, the
young leaves of Arizona ash, *Fraxinus velutina,* are covered
with fuzz (it wears off later as they mature).

venation
The way in which veins are arranged, usually on a leaf.

Verbascum
The botanical name for mullein.

veris or *vernalis*

As a species name, means "flowering in early spring," as do cowslip, *Primula veris,* and Ozark witch hazel, *Hamamelis vernalis.*

vermiculite

A micaceous mineral, heated until it explodes into spongelike kernels that are highly porous but exceedingly lightweight. It is a component of some soilless mixes.

vernalization

The exposure to several weeks of cool temperatures that is required by some plants to initiate bud formation or new growth.

Veronia

The botanical name for ironweed.

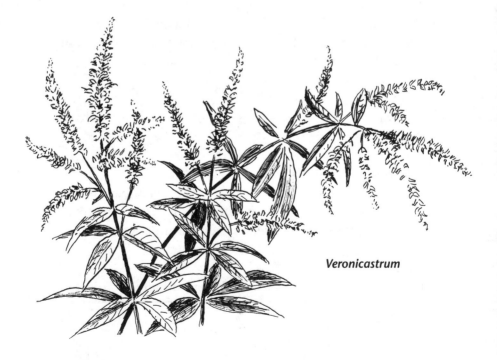

Veronicastrum

Veronicastrum
The botanical name for Culver's root.

verruculosus, -a, -um
As a species name, means "warty." For example, warty barberry, *Berberis verruculosa,* has wartlike bumps on its twigs.

verticillatus, -a, -um
As a species name, means "with leaves arranged in whorls." For example, threadleaf coreopsis, *Coreopsis verticillata,* has whorls of very thin, needlelike leaves.

verticillium
A common soilborne fungal disease that affects a wide variety of plants, causing wilting or death. *See also* V,F,N.

V,F,N
A designation on packages of vegetable seeds or in catalogs. One or more of these letters indicate that the plant is resistant to, respectively, verticillium wilt, fusarium wilt, or certain nematodes — or all three.

viability
The capacity of a seed to germinate. Some seeds remain viable for a very short time, others for decades or even centuries. Also called seed viability.

victory garden
During World War II, a vegetable garden made by homeowners to grow their own food crops and thus support the war effort.

vigor
Strong healthy growth and the ability to withstand stress.

villosus, -a, -um
As a species name, means "covered with soft hairs." For example, feathertop, *Pennisetum villosum,* has fluffy white seed heads.

Vinca
The botanical name for periwinkle.

Vinca

vine
Any plant, whether woody or herbaceous, with slender climbing or trailing stems. It may climb by tendrils, twining, or holdfasts or simply run along the ground.

Viola
The botanical name for pansy and violet.

-virens or virid-
As part of a species name, means "green." For example, green hellebore, *Helleborus viridis,* has green flowers.

virgatus, -a, -um
As a species name, means "having a twiggy appearance" but is usually applied to herbaceous, not woody, plants. For

example, switch grass, *Panicum virgatum,* has stiff, twiggy flower stalks.

virginicus, -a, -um or *virginiana*

As a species name, means "native to Virginia" but is also used for plants from that general area. Many plants native throughout the eastern United States, such as eastern red cedar, *Juniperus virginiana,* were first collected and named in Virginia.

viridescence

The process by which variegated leaves revert to all-green.

virus

A type of disease organism that causes a streaky discoloration of leaves or petals, distorts buds and new growth, and weakens plants.

viscosus, -a, -um

As a species name, means "sticky." For example, the summer-blooming swamp azalea, *Rhododendron viscosum,*

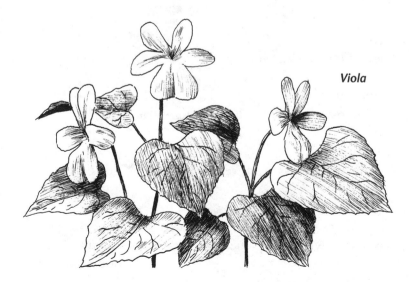

Viola

has white flowers that smell very sweet but feel surprisingly sticky.

Vitex
The botanical name for chaste tree.

viticulture
The growing of grapevines for fruit or winemaking.

Vitis

Vitis
The botanical name for grape.

viviparous
Bearing plantlets on the leaves, stems, or flowers.

volunteer
A plant that grows from self-sown seed.

vulgaris, -e
As a species name, means "common," as in the common privet so often used for hedges, *Ligustrum vulgare.*

Waimea Arboretum and Botanical Garden
An institution located 35 miles from Honolulu. In its 30 different botanical collections, the emphasis is on threatened tropical plants as well as on Hawaiian natives.

wall garden
A collection or display of plants grown in the spaces between the rocks of a dry stone wall.

Wardian case
An airtight enclosed glass case, invented in 1833 by Dr. Nathanial Ward, a plant collector, who was the first to succeed in transporting live plants over great distances (in his case, between Australia and England). The Wardian case revolutionized plant collecting and became a popular feature in Victorian living rooms. The terrarium, or bottle garden, is a modern version.

warm-season grass
A grass that grows most vigorously at temperatures above 70 to 80 degrees F and goes dormant in cool weather. Warm-season grasses include Bermudagrass and St. Augustine grass. Pampas grass and fountain grass are warm-season ornamental grasses. *See also* **cool-season grass**.

Washington Park Arboretum
A Seattle institution noted for its extraordinary collection
of more than 5,000 woody plants that grow in the Puget
Sound area. It also contains an authentic Japanese garden,
whose crowning feature is a 200-year-old Kobe lantern.

water garden
Any ornamental tub, pool, or other natural or artificial
water container planted with aquatic plants.

watershoot
See watersprout.

watersprout
An undesirable, very vigorous vertical shoot that forms on
trees, usually in response to severe pruning. Also called
watershoot.

Wave Hill
The former home at various times of Mark Twain,
Theodore Roosevelt, and Arturo Toscanini, located in the
Riverdale section of New York City. Occupying a
spectacular site overlooking the Hudson River, it is
considered one of the most beautiful public gardens in the
United States, notable for its "unpublic garden" look.

weed
1. According to Emerson, "a plant whose virtues have not
   yet been discovered." A less generous but more useful
   definition from the *American Heritage Dictionary* calls a
   weed "a plant considered undesirable, unattractive, or
   troublesome, especially one growing where it is not
   wanted, as in a garden."
2. The stems and leaves of a plant, as opposed to its seeds,
   as in "dill weed."

weevil

(actual size)

weeping
Having drooping branches.

weevil
Any of several garden beetle pests that feed on all parts of plants, typically most active at night.

wet feet
Root damage in potted plants caused by excessive watering and insufficient drainage.

wettable powder
A substance that does not dissolve in water but remains suspended in it. Usually refers to pesticides that are applied as sprays.

wetting agent
See **surfactant**.

whitefly

↝
(actual size)

whip
A young unbranched shoot of a woody plant, especially the first year's growth from a graft or bud.

whitefly
A tiny mothlike insect that feeds on sap. Whiteflies are particularly troublesome in greenhouses or in warm climates.

whorl
A group of three or more leaves or shoots that emerge from a single node.

wide-row gardening
An efficient way of spacing plants, popular in vegetable or cutting gardens, by grouping them in wide rows or beds about 2 to 3 feet wide, rather than lining them out single file.

wildflower
A native or exotic plant that grows wild in a region and has conspicuous flowers.

Wilson, E. H. (Ernest Henry) (1876–1930)
English-born and -educated horticulturist who became assistant director of Harvard's Arnold Arboretum. A famous plant hunter, he traveled extensively in the Orient and introduced the regal lily and other Oriental plants to Western gardens.

wilt
A plant disease caused by either bacteria or fungi. Some wilts are carried by beetles or other insects.

windbreak
One or more rows of closely spaced trees or hedges positioned to lessen the force of the wind and shelter a garden or house. Also called shelter belt.

windfall
Ripe or near-ripe fruit that falls to the ground.

window box
Traditionally, a long planter attached to a building just beneath a window.

wind-pollinated
Having the pollen carried by the wind instead of by insects. Wind-pollinated plants include pines, birches, grasses, and many others.

wing
A thin flat extension found at the margins of a seed or leafstalk or along a stem.

winterkill
The dieback of twigs in winter because the wood was not sufficiently hardened to withstand severe weather or because the plant is not hardy enough for the site.

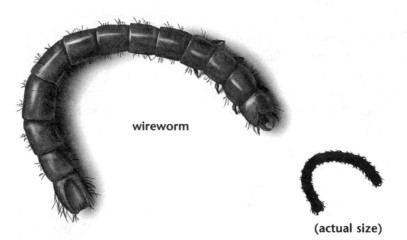

wireworm

(actual size)

Winterthur
The former home of Henry Francis du Pont, located outside of Wilmington, Delaware. The 200 acres of gardens, designed by du Pont, are one of the finest examples in the United States of landscaping in the naturalistic English style. They are typical of the large country estates in the early 20th century.

wireworm
A shiny orange or brown grub that feeds on many vegetable crops as well as on gladiolus corms.

Wisley
See **Royal Horticultural Society.**

witches' broom
A thickly congested, pincushion-like growth of branches that appears on a tree, presumably in response to insect or viral damage. Cuttings taken from these branches usually result in dwarf plants.

wood
The secondary xylem or tough inner core of a tree, shrub, or perennial vine.

woody perennial

A plant that lives for more than a year, has hard rather than fleshy stems, and bears buds that survive above ground in winter. Trees, shrubs, many vines, and bamboos are examples of woody perennials. *See also* **herbaceous perennial.**

woolly adelgid

A mealybug-like insect that attacks hemlock trees.

wort

An Old English word for a plant. Often used in combination, as in milkwort or liverwort.

Wyman, Donald (1904–1993)

For 35 years, horticulturist of the Arnold Arboretum, and an expert on hardy woody plants. His primary function was the introduction of new plants to the arboretum and thus to the United States. In one year, he brought back seeds or plants of 930 species. His major book was *Wyman's Gardening Encyclopedia,* published in 1971.

witches'
broom

xanth-

As part of a species name, means "yellow." For example, yellowroot, *Xanthorhiza simplicissima,* is a low shrub with yellow roots.

Xeriscape

From the Greek *xeros,* which means "dry," a water-conserving landscape design. Xeriscaping, as a word and a style, was developed in the early 1980s by the Denver Water Department as a way to landscape in an area that has chronic water shortages.

xylem

The water-conducting tissue of plants. *See also* **phloem**.

Xeriscape

Zantedeschia
The botanical name for calla.

Zen garden
A style of Japanese gardening based on the contemplative gardens in the courtyards of the Zen temples during the 16th century. Zen gardens are minimalist creations in which raked sand and a few well-placed stones are the primary features.

Zephyranthes
The botanical name for zephyr flower.

zone
See **hardiness zones; climate zones.**

zygomorphic
A term used to describe an irregular flower with bilateral symmetry. Common examples are snapdragons, foxgloves, and all orchids. *See also* **actinomorphic; irregular flower.**

Titles available in the Taylor's Guide series:

Taylor's Guide to Annuals	$19.95
Taylor's Guide to Perennials	22.00
Taylor's Guide to Roses, Revised Edition	19.95
Taylor's Guide to Bulbs	23.00
Taylor's Guide to Ground Covers	23.00
Taylor's Guide to Houseplants	19.95
Taylor's Guide to Vegetables	19.95
Taylor's Guide to Shrubs	23.00
Taylor's Guide to Trees	19.95
Taylor's Guide to Garden Design	19.95
Taylor's Guide to Water-Saving Gardening	19.95
Taylor's Guide to Garden Techniques	19.95
Taylor's Guide to Gardening in the South	19.95
Taylor's Guide to Gardening in the Southwest	19.95
Taylor's Guide to Natural Gardening	19.95
Taylor's Guide to Specialty Nurseries	16.95
Taylor's Guide to Shade Gardening	19.95
Taylor's Guide to Herbs	19.95
Taylor's Guide to Container Gardening	19.95
Taylor's Guide to Heirloom Vegetables	19.95
Taylor's Guide to Fruits and Berries	19.95
Taylor's Guide to Orchids	24.00
Taylor's Guide to Seashore Gardening	19.95
Taylor's Guide to Ornamental Grasses	19.95
Taylor's Master Guide to Gardening	60.00

At your bookstore or by calling 1-800-225-3362

Prices subject to change without notice